FULL OF LOVE

Mom-to-mom advice for enriching families with
simple photo albums and scrapbooking

NANCY O'DELL

FULL OF LOVE

Creative Memories
3001 Clearwater Road
St. Cloud, MN 56301
(800) 468-9335
www.creativememories.com

ISBN 978-061539890-7

Designed by Creative Memories.

Photography by Ulrica Wihlborg Photography (www.ulricawihlborg.com), pages 12, 28, 29, 34, 40, 44, 45, 50, 55, 56, 58, 59, 61, 63-67, 69, 71, 72, 74-90, 114-141, 144-157, 160-163, 168, 169, covers.
Photography by kc kratt photography (www.kckratt.com), pages 31, 169.
Photography by Adventure Studios – John Linn (www.adventureadvertising.com), pages 30, 73, 167.
Photography by Them Too Photography – Angela Calero / Alain Uy (www.themtoo.com), pages 51, 94, 95.
Photography by John Solano Photography (www.imagemakr.com), pages 22 (wedding only), 104, 105.
Photography by Scott Garfield – ©American Broadcasting Companies, Inc., page 108.
Photography by Scott Boardman, page 54.
Photography by Brian Knox Photography, pages 49, 158, 159.
Photography by Feeling Productions – Richard Gauthier, pages 110, 111.

TABLE OF CONTENTS

ACKNOWLEDGEMENTS

OF ALL THE PEOPLE I HAVE TO THANK for their part in making this book a reality, the first is my mom, Betty. Through her photographs and her passion for scrapbooking, my mother shared her love for me in a lasting and important way. Literally, I was able to hold in my hands the proof that I was soooo very loved as a child. Even in her passing, my mother has made my sister and I feel like the most cherished children in the world. Thanks, Mom, for being the most cherished mother in the world.

Next, my Grandmom. She instilled the passion for scrapbooking in my mother through her own album-making, which had been shared with her by her father. Because of them, I even have a beautiful love letter he wrote to my great-grandmother when they were "courting" in the late 1890s. Knowing that I come from a family with such a loving legacy is priceless.

The first gift my husband Keith gave me was a scrapbook, in which he'd documented all the places we'd visited together and the things we'd done during our courtship. It is still the best gift I've ever received. Every time I look at it I fall even more in love with him. Thank you, Babe, for knowing me so well, and for cherishing our memories as much as I do. I love you.

To my stepsons Carson and Tyler. Thank you for sharing your stories with me. I'll always remember the looks on your faces when I gave you your very first scrapbooks. In making those, I got to know you even better – as the babies and toddlers you were before I met you as little boys. I love being your "Nommy" and am so honored you and your precious selves are now a part of OUR story.

And my baby girl, Ashby. Thank you for giving me … everything. Seeing the world through your eyes is the most precious gift I can imagine, and it connects me even more profoundly to my own mother. I hope the scrapbooks I pass on to you will also make you feel so very loved. Because you are.

After my mother passed away, my father, knowing how much her scrapbooks and albums meant to me, gave them to me. Thank you, Dad, for that gift, and for being the hands-down most wonderful father in the world.

To my big sister, Karen. Thanks for giving me the great comfort of knowing that, as sisters, we'll always be there for each other. I can't think of anyone with whom I'd rather share all those pages in Mom's albums.

To Mama and Papa Z. What a lucky girl I am to have you as parents-in-law! Thanks for always being there when we need a little extra help and love.

There are so many people involved in a project like this. I was fortunate enough to have talented people not just involved, but committed. (Even though one or two of them probably felt about ready to have themselves committed as we raced down the homestretch!) To each of them, I say thank you. You've all demonstrated professionalism and dedication throughout this journey we've taken together.

Meryl Michon, my senior producer, who's been on every conference call, copied on every email and helped coordinate everything. You know my life better than I do. Without a doubt, Meryl, this wouldn't have been possible without you.

To Ulrica Wihlborg and Dr. Condrell. Thanks so much for sharing your wonderful wisdom and advice. I hope other families find just as much inspiration in it as I have. And to Dave Kirchner, who helped me take what was in my heart and put it into words. I loved our conversations.

Rhonda Anderson, who founded this wonderful company called Creative Memories. The value of what you have done in sharing the importance of memory-keeping with the world is immeasurable. I am humbled and honored to work with you in this mission.

Karen Thompson, Creative Director; Corinne Skoog, Art Director and Greg Skoog, Editor. Thank you for the countless hours of hard work you poured into this project. It wouldn't be as beautiful and meaningful without you.

Loren Castronovo, Creative Memories Vice President of Marketing. Thank you for being so inspirational, for believing in me and for so warmly drawing me into the Creative Memories family. I am so grateful to have gotten to know you and the beautiful person you are.

John Dinan, who coordinated everything between Creative Memories and me. You are one of the most organized people I've ever met – amazing! It has been an absolute joy to work with you.

Chris Veit, Creative Memories CEO. Thank you for allowing me to be part of the Creative Memories story. Your team is amazing, organized and filled with genuine people. I know that starts at the top, so thank you.

My make-it-happen trio in L.A., Joe P., Lizzy and Julie. For all your encouragement, the countless weekend hours spent scanning photos, your help digging through hundreds of pictures, and for doing everything else I didn't have time to do … thank you.

Can't forget Joe S. Thanks for your willingness to always help when I need you. Love ya "little brother"!

To my manager, Mark Schulman, and my endorsement agent, Brooke Slavik-Jung. Thank you for helping this project come to fruition. You're the best.

To Garth. Sometimes it feels awkward to ask a busy friend for a favor. When that person makes you feel as if it is an honor to help you, then you know that is a real friend! Indeed, you are a true friend. Thanks for always being there, G!

Annie Jeeves, my publicist. Thanks to your work on our first book, *Full of Life*, this opportunity came to be. Thank you, thank you, thank you for not only doing your job well, but for caring. Love ya!

To all of the wonderful, talented, dedicated Creative Memories Consultants who have so graciously welcomed me into the CM family. It's an honor for me to be a part of what you do because I feel what you do is so important.

And to everyone at the Creative Memories Home Office, including Jill Kampa, Melissa Ullmann, Pam Cesnik, Addie Rysavy, Jen Lessinger, Ginger Williams, Jenny Dammann and Karen Hengel. From the bottom of my heart, thank you for everything.

Special thanks to all of the friends, family members and celebrities who allowed me to share their photos and words in this book and for putting up with my need to snap photos for my scrapbook albums for so many years. Say cheese! And thank you for the great memories throughout so many years!

FOREWORD

"FOUNDATION." Dictionaries define the word as a "basis" or "nucleus." All will stress its importance. Nancy O'Dell defines "foundation" in one word: family.

One of the greatest feelings in life is to belong. One of the fastest growing tragedies in life is the fragmentation of families. Nancy believes one of the greatest gifts we can give our children is the importance of family ... the entire family. Through scrapbooking, Nancy will give her children a gift that is irreplaceable, invaluable and the most loving gift a parent can give. She's giving her kids a foundation.

Nancy gets it. As a mother to her daughter and as a "bonus mom" to her two wonderful stepsons, Nancy knows motherhood from all sides. As a loving daughter, Nancy cherishes the photos of family members who came before her and wants to pass along the gift of her dear mother's love to her own children. Within these pages are easy tips and ideas to follow to create your own family's foundation for generations to come.

Though she was raised on common sense and was always the girl next door, it was easy to see there was something special about Nancy. I first met her as we were both stepping into entertainment. And after two decades of

Garth Brooks was one of my first celebrity interviews in 1996. Through the years we've become great friends. I call Garth "the real deal" and a true friend. That's why he's made so many pages in my scrapbooks!

the biggest award shows, the biggest names in Hollywood and the biggest stories from around the world, I can attest Nancy is that same girl and still has that common sense. I applaud her choice to invest her time in her family and I tip my hat to her for recognizing there is no better way to remind your children they are a part of something bigger – something permanent – and something that is always there ... family.

INTRODUCTION

I HAVE A SECRET. OK, well it's not really a deep, dark secret that I keep hidden. (To tell the truth, it's a part of my life of which I'm really proud!) It's just something that a lot of people don't know about me.

And it's something that, when folks find out... Well, I think my dear friend Holly Robinson Peete's reaction summed it up best.

Holly's one of the first girlfriends I made in Hollywood. Here we are back in 1997. Love her and we relate on so many different levels. Scrapbooking, however, was a level which took a while to sink in!

"Girl, you got time for what?!"

You see, I'm a scrapbooker.

Now, to some people, "scrapbooking" means spending hours cutting out shapes from construction paper and messing with smelly paste. And it scares the tar out of them. So I guess I should be clear. I use the word "scrapbook." And, to me, the books I make are absolutely beautiful. But the heart of my photo albums will always be pictures and stories, not bells and whistles.

For that reason, one of my scrapbooking heroes has always been Rhonda Anderson – one of the co-founders of Creative Memories. She's kind of been scrapbooking's version of a rock star for the last 25 years with her no-frills message of "simple pages ... completed albums." (Just like Mom used to make 'em!)

So when I got the chance to talk with Rhonda, I was excited. And as I talked with everyone at Creative Memories, I could feel a partnership coming on. And it has! We're developing products that are beautiful – but that offer easy options to keep from overwhelming the busy parents of this world. The first batch is my Hummingbird Series. It's available now and it's something I feel passionate about! I truly believe that albums have the power to change lives.

And then it hit me. The last time I felt this passionately about something, I ended up writing a book about it: *Full of Life – Mom-to-Mom Tips I Wish Someone Had Told Me When I Was Pregnant.*

I was blessed with a mother who knew how important albums can be in making children feel loved, valued and confident. So photo albums have always been part of my life. And over the course of my career, I've become an expert at finding ways to fit album-making into the cracks of a busy life.

I realized I have to share that. So this book includes my tips, my stories, my advice and my recommendations. But it's more than that. Because, over the years, I've stumbled onto a surprisingly simple formula:

Better Stories + Better Photos = Better Albums

You have great stories in you. (Trust me. Everyone does!) I'll share some of the techniques I've learned from interviewing on the red carpet that have carried over into my albums and made the stories I tell in them come to life. For the other half of the equation, I'll turn to professional lifestyle photographer Ulrica Wihlborg to get the scoop on all the simple little things we can do to kick our photos up a notch.

And, since the reporter in me always wondered if the albums I cherished as a little girl truly were as influential in my upbringing as I always believed they were, I'll quiz noted child psychologist Dr. Kenneth Condrell to find out. I think his answers will amaze you.

OUR ALBUMS
So Much More Than Pictures on a Page

*"Blessed are the children of scrapbookers,
for they shall inherit the scrapbooks."*
—*Author Unknown*

THE RED CARPET IS FULL OF SURPRISES. Lighting rigs fall. Sprinkler systems go off. Teleprompters stop working. Now don't get me wrong – it's a wonderful, glamorous place to work. And, after 13 years of co-hosting *Access Hollywood* and doing live Golden Globe and Emmy Arrival shows, I can truly say I've loved it. But rolling with the surprises and boldly flagging down the people who viewers want to hear from takes a healthy sense of self-assurance.

I'm not talking about cockiness, but rather a simple and quiet confidence. And I thank my mother for giving me that security. No, she didn't pass along some special chromosome. She merely showed me a whole lot of love. Fifty-three albums' worth, actually.

Those albums picked me up, got me by, made me laugh and made me cry. And, having been raised with them in my life, I can't imagine life without them.

So I keep the tradition of scrapbooking in my family alive and well. And you'd be surprised at some of the looks I get for it. Honestly, when I mention my albums to some friends, you'd think I told them I was an undercover operative for the CIA!

Say cheese! (No, don't say cheese. That never really works. So why do people keep saying it, and where did it come from anyway?!) People like Tom Hanks, Jamie Foxx and Al Roker have their pictures taken all the time. So I'm always humbled and grateful when they're so happy to take the time for a personal shot for my albums. These truly are some of the nicest people I know!

Actually, come to think of it, there have been times when I really was scrap-booking undercover! On the *Access* set, on movie sets, at screenings, and even on the red carpet at the *Oscars*, when there was downtime, I'd slip off to a little corner somewhere, whip out the supplies I'd brought in my bag and get a few pages done. (Scrapbooking in an evening gown – so much fun!)

Celebrities like Tom Hanks, Madonna, Leonardo DiCaprio, Garth Brooks and Jamie Foxx have all been more than gracious in posing for many a picture. As for my longtime pal Al Roker, who's been my co-host for the *Tournament of Roses Parade* these past 10 years, our annual album photo together has become something of a tradition.

So, as surprised and curious as they are when I tell them, it seems that the more I talk about my scrapbooks and the more people see how much they mean to me, the more honored they seem to feel when I ask them to pose for a picture.

When I found out I was pregnant with my baby girl, Ashby, I wanted to put together an album of all the celebrities she got to meet when she was still in my belly. So, after my husband, Madonna was one of the first to know I was pregnant. (I whispered it to her at eight weeks when I asked her for a picture for my pregnancy album.) It's amazing the hour-long interviews you suddenly get when you tell a celebrity you're with child!

And it was kind of funny because some of the stars would actually get a little self-conscious and ask for "photo approval" after I'd taken the shot. Now, these are stars whose pictures are out there everywhere. But once they knew the photo was going into Ashby's scrapbook, forever and ever, it was for real. ("Um, can I just check and make sure I don't look goofy or anything?")

Madonna was one of the first people I told that I was pregnant with Ashby. At the time of this photo, she had recently adopted her son, David. What a nice interview we had as fellow mothers, and what a beautiful side of Madonna! That's why this is my favorite photo with her – because it reminds me of that nice day!

Very sweet. And as I think of the celebrities who were the most surprised when I told them I was a scrapper, when their eyes went wide and their jaws dropped, the following are the 'fraid-to-say-it questions that lots of them had ... but few would actually ask.

*　*　*

Isn't scrapbooking kind of dated?
Well, on some level, that's the idea, isn't it? When I look back at some of the big hair and hypercolor sweatshirts in my albums from ... a few years ago, it's like a time machine. Sure, it makes me cringe. But it also makes me smile.

More importantly though, albums are filled with timeless moments that make up your life. Let me share a wonderful example.

I love to capture simple, everyday moments in my albums. But, of course, you've got to have the big milestones in there too! My albums just wouldn't feel the same without fantastic rites of passage like my college freshman portrait (love the hair ... NOT!) and college graduation. (Go Clemson Tigers!)

In one of my albums I have a picture of me with legendary news anchor, Diane Sawyer. It's one I took in 1993 when I made my very first trip to the Big Apple. I was living in Charleston, South Carolina, where I'd taken my first full-time job as a reporter, and I still wasn't totally sure that was what I wanted to do for the rest of my life. But in New York, a friend got me in to watch the taping of an ABC News segment.

Now, I'd always thought Diane Sawyer came across as incredibly intelligent and genuine on the air. But in person – oh gosh, she took my breath away. She was so generous with her time, and her words of encouragement made me feel as if I could do absolutely anything I set my mind to. I remember thinking, *How is it possible that someone so smart and so talented could also be so nice?*

I still feel so blessed and lucky to have met Diane Sawyer way back in 1993. Her advice and kindness really did help set me on the right path.

That was a career turning point for me. It was when I truly made up my mind: *I'll have what she's having!*

The picture of the two of us together is so precious to me because it's a reminder of a day that forever changed my life. If I hadn't met Diane Sawyer that afternoon in New York City, I might not have stayed in broadcasting and made the move to Miami, where I started working for NBC, which eventually led to my job on *Access Hollywood* in Los Angeles. And if I hadn't been living in L.A., I for sure wouldn't have met my husband Keith, the love of my life, in that airport security line in 2004. And I wouldn't have the two incredible stepsons with whom I've been blessed and the beautiful baby girl my husband and I had together, the light of my life, Ashby!

Isn't scrapbooking just so much work?

I always tell people I can make 10 album pages in 10 minutes or less and they can too. Now, it definitely helps when you've already got great stories and photos up your sleeve (more on those later), but here are some of the other things I do.

Number one, I *make* time to make my albums, and it doesn't have to be a lot of time. Whether it's once a week, once every couple of weeks or once a month – I'll just schedule it like it's a hair appointment. If you let boxes and boxes of photos pile up, it's going to seem like it's difficult. And believe me, album-making should *not* be difficult.

I also multitask. I'll take a few pages with me in my bag so I can work on them between takes at a photo shoot. (You'd be surprised how much waiting around goes on at a photo shoot!) When I'm home, I'm almost always scrapping with my baby girl. It's one of the best ways we spend time together. And the photos let me tell her family stories and even teach her things, from colors to counting: *What color shirt is Mommy wearing there? How many flowers are in this picture?* Every child loves a storybook. So why not make it a personal one, filled with their favorite things? Pictures!

Plus, I look at making albums as a series of baby steps I can do over time. That way I'm never overwhelmed thinking I have to do it all at once. It starts when I print my photos. I write the date on the back of each one (no ballpoint pens!), then I sort them into plain white 8x10 envelopes by how I think I'll use them – usually by event. I'll write myself little reminders on the envelopes about something somebody said that day or the one thing I want to be sure I journal about. Even if I don't get around to making the pages right away, those envelopes and those notes give me a huge head start when I finally do. They almost turn making the album into an assembly-line process.

Now, I started out organizing my photos in plain ol' envelopes (and I still like to use them). But there are amazing products out there today to help you organize. I especially like the Creative Memories Power® Sort Box. I use it right alongside my envelopes, and they both work great for me.

In fact, for all of the Creative Memories tools and products that make putting together an album so much easier, I have to stop right here and give a shout-out of thanks to my wonderful friend, Rhonda Anderson. Whenever we get together and talk about our albums, it's her spirit and her sense of purpose that never fail to recharge my batteries. She faithfully reminds

Creative Memories Co-founder Rhonda Anderson – love her! For years, she's been telling the world what I've known all my life. Photo albums have the power to change lives.

me: *It's all about the stories on the page.* Hard to believe it's coming up on 25 years since Rhonda co-founded Creative Memories and put scrapbooking on the map!

And when it comes to mapping out scrapbooks, I do that in baby steps too. If I'm under the gun, I might just put down my photos in one session, then go back and add the borders and the stickers and all the froufrou later. Even when I think I'm done journaling, I'll sometimes slap down an extra blank journaling box because there's always *something* I forgot to say.

I like to think of my albums as works in progress. When you do that, it gives you this tremendous sense of freedom and takes away so much pressure. Since you know you can go back anytime and make your pages even better, you never hesitate to start making them in the first place. You get your albums done.

But I think the most important thing I do is just keep scrapping. I'm like the Energizer Bunny that way. No matter how organized you are, at some time or another, you're gonna have pictures pile up that you "keep meaning to get to." I sure do. But you know what? I just remind myself that I will get to them eventually and go right back to capturing the memories that are happening right now.

I mean, who said you have to scrap in chronological order? Keep moving forward and make some pages with the pictures you shot last weekend. I never want to let those "yesterday photos" I haven't gotten around to stand in the way of all the wonderful pages I can make today. Just get started!

Isn't she lovely? Thanks to her albums, I have page after page of amazing insights into the beautiful dreamer who grew up to be my mom. That's her high school graduation invitation on the left. And the big, "Gone With the Wind" picture of her as a young girl is one of my all-time favorites!

What was it that got you started in scrapbooking?

Well that could be a whole 'nother book, because my family's scrapbooking history goes back four generations. I only have to go back one generation though – to my wonderful mom, Betty.

As I grew up, her bedroom closet was piled high with the scrapbooks she'd made about me and my big sis, Karen. She would spread out photos on her bed and just start putting them down on the pages. And she wouldn't stop till she was finished. It didn't take long for her to fill up an album because she didn't add the pictures in any kind of order. I mean, you might see a picture of me in college on this page and one of me as a baby on the next. It was true stream-of-consciousness scrapbooking!

But that's one of the things I love about those albums. I'm glad she didn't fuss over this and that, because if she had, those albums might never have gotten made.

And I will never forget the first time I saw how important those albums could be. I was in the first grade, and I had this kitty cat I absolutely adored. Well, come to find out, my sister had developed an allergy to cats. And so my cat had to go. It was when I asked Mom if we could give away Karen instead of the cat that she decided, *OK. Time to break out the scrapbooks!*

We sat down and she showed me pictures of me with pet cats going back to when I was just a toddler. She told me how I was always so loving to them, and that was good because being kind to animals is important. Then she pointed to pictures of me when I was a teeny little baby and pictures of my sister and me growing up. She said Karen had been there by my side since my very first day and that she would always be there for me – much more than any kitty cat would ever be.

Now just so you know, I tell my sister to this very day that I would never, ever trade her for a cat! But until I got that first glimpse of the magic that albums can do, that day was a different story.

My sister Karen and I shared a lot of things as we were growing up – including more album pages than I can count. And, for the record, I'd still never trade her for a cat.

In the space of just a few minutes, Mom had used this simple scrapbook to fill in memories of my early childhood that I could never recall on my own, since I was so young when they happened. And at the same time, she taught me about the deep bonds our family has.

I wondered how this little book from the corner drug store could do all that. Well, the lessons I learned from that little book were far from over. Not long after, Mom brought it out again when she sat me down on her bed and said, *"My sweet Nancy, your great-grandmother, Mimi, passed away last night. You're not gonna get to see her again."*

I didn't really have any concept of death at that time, but I know I started crying. Through my tears, I could see Mom turning the pages of that scrapbook and pointing to pictures of me with Mimi as I was growing up. She showed me pictures of her house and pictures of me, Mimi and the family celebrating a holiday over a family meal. Mom said that even though

I would never see Mimi again, she would always be looking over me, and she would always be part of my life because she'd always be part of my memories.

Of course she was right. The first time a child loses a loved one – oh my gosh, the pain. But looking back, thanks to Mom and those scrapbooks, I can see just how much the photos, and the memories they brought back, helped me get through it all.

I don't remember everything about the times I spent with Mimi, as I was so young. But, thanks to albums, I know a lot about her and I have a deep sense of connection to my great-grandmother. And the one strong memory I do have every time I look at a photo of her is of the love we shared.

And right around the time Ashby celebrated her first birthday, I sat down with *my* daughter on my bed to have a similar talk. I pulled out our scrapbooks and we looked at all the happy pictures of her with her Grandmama Betty.

Yes, my wonderful mother, Betty, lost her battle with ALS, Lou Gehrig's disease. It is one of the toughest things I have ever been through, as she was my best friend, and I couldn't have asked for a better mother. Her family was her life, and I never doubted for a second that she and my dad would be there for anything I ever needed. And I have the albums to prove it. What a wonderful feeling that is to have as a child and to be reminded of years later as an adult!

Knowing that I shared the same passion for scrapbooking as my mother, my father gave me her albums when she passed away. As I look through all 53 of them, page by page, I feel so connected to my mom. Through the memories in those albums, I get to relive our great times all over again.

That same connection I have to my great-grandmother is what I dream of for Ashby and my mother. Years from now Ashby may not remember all the hugs and kisses Grandma Betty showered on her. But she will grow up knowing just who Grandma Betty was and just how much she loved her!

And I discovered that, even though it was so difficult for her to use her hands because of the way ALS destroys muscles, Mom still scrapped *everything* I sent her about my baby girl – from pregnancy to birth – every ultrasound photo, every Post-It note, every article I sent her and, of course, every photo of Ashby. And, while looking at those albums makes me miss my mom, they do show me how fortunate I was that she was able to meet Ashby and to see her grow for nearly a full year. Her albums show me how Mom was determined to have her baby granddaughter feel her love, despite the fact that ALS had made it difficult for her to even pucker her lips.

I'll never forget that. And thanks to the albums, Ashby will always know it too.

*　　*　　*

Picture of Your Baby
♥ ♥Granddaughter ♥♥
To Come!!

Even as ALS progressively took her away from us, Mom continued to save everything in her albums

My mother was a very special woman – bound and determined to make everyone feel loved. And even today, after her passing, she's still helping others through Betty's Battle (www.bettysbattle.org), a charity founded in her honor to help find a cure for ALS.

WHENEVER YOU MOVE, you always find things you forgot you had. And sometimes those things turn out to be priceless. When Keith and I moved into our new home, I found boxes of pictures that he'd carefully stored away. They were of his sons, Carson and Tyler – my new stepsons – as they were growing up. Well, I knew right away what I had to do with *those!*

As I made my boys' scrapbooks from those found-photo treasures, I had so much fun looking at all the pictures and learning so much about them. I gave the finished albums to them as Christmas presents. And when they opened them up and comprehended what they were, the looks on their faces showed me how much the gift meant to them. And then, when we all started flipping through the pages together, did the questions ever fly!

As a child, the first times I saw pictures of tiny little me in a scrapbook, I remember wanting to know absolutely everything that was going on and who all these people were. I'd ask Mom and Dad and Grandmom – *Who is that?*

A few years ago, in a delightfully fateful airport security line, I met one wonderful man. That was lucky. But getting two more wonderful men in my life at the same time? That was amazing! Carson and Tyler are very special guys. And I hope their albums always remind them that's exactly how I feel!

Where were we? Why was I crying? Now here it is so many years later, and I'm doing the exact same thing. Only this time I'm the mom asking my step-sons all the questions – *What was that award for? When were you guys in Hawaii? How come you've got that goofy look on your face?*

That day, those album pages – they gave the three of us something rare. It was the chance to bond over things that had happened in our lives from before we ever knew one other. But those things are now shared memories. They're part of the history of our new family.

When you become part of a blended family as we all did, there's this distance you have to bridge. Stepparents and stepkids really want to connect with each other. They just don't always know how. Those albums became our bridge.

The other thing those albums did? Without a single word being spoken, they told Carson and Tyler exactly how much they mean to me. That's really what our albums are for, you know – to say "I love you." No, I take that back. *To shout it!*

For sure, the scrapbooks Mom made schooled me about life lessons and family values. But what I'll always remember most about them is the unspoken "I love you" that came flying off every page. Seeing all the little things Mom kept as I grew up – things I never in a million years would have imagined she'd save – and then reading the tender words she wrote about them.... How could I *not* feel like I was the most loved child in the whole world?

Her albums, my albums, your albums ... they're chock-full of pictures, words, memorabilia and lots of beautiful things to show them all off. But the only ingredient that really matters, the only reason we make them in the first place – they're *full of love!*

KIDS AND PHOTOS
They Just Click

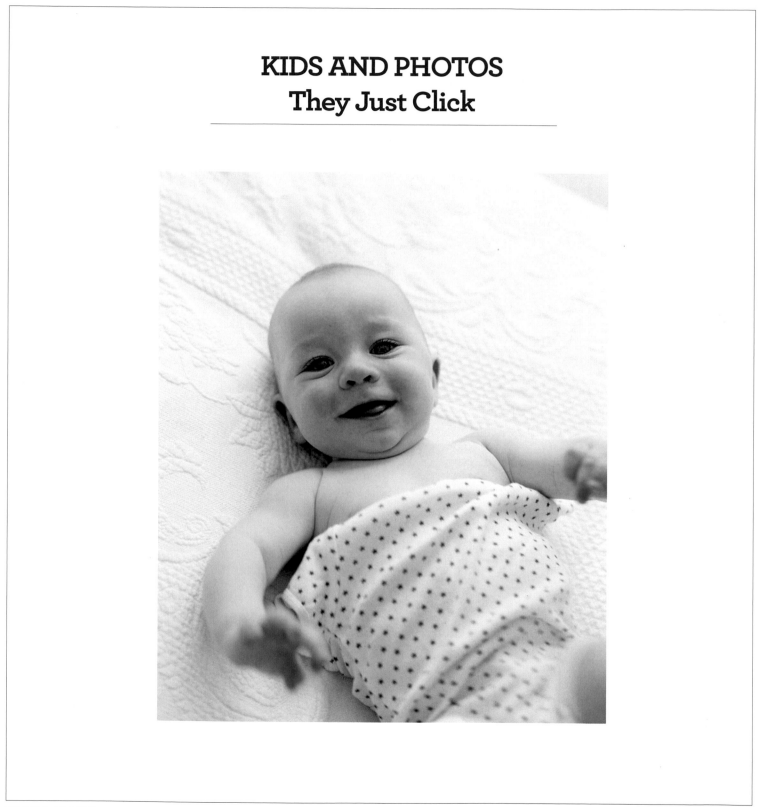

"Looking through some photographs I found inside a drawer, I was taken by a photograph of you."

—*Jackson Browne*

I CAN'T TELL YOU how much Mom's photos meant to me growing up. I don't think I fully realized it at the time, but those photos and the albums she put them in became part of my DNA – always there in the back of my mind. And sometimes they were almost like a life preserver that got tossed out to me whenever I needed it most. If something went wrong at school, all I had to do was think back on an album page Mom made about a day when everything went right at school. Right then and there, I could put that pesky little setback behind me.

And most of all, I could see it for the pesky little setback it was!

Those albums Mom made were living proof of all the values and traditions our family held dear. They showed off all the good times we'd shared ... and some of the rough times too.

Naturally, the reporter in me wondered if my experience was somehow special. How *do* family photos and scrapbooks play a part in the way we grow up?

To find out, I sat down with Dr. Kenneth Condrell, nationally known child psychologist, family counselor and author. What I learned was a real eye-opener. Before, I pretty much thought I had scrapbooking down pat. I mean, I'd already made so doggone many of them!

But thanks to Dr. Condrell, I had the 'aha' moment for which I'd been waiting. He not only validated my belief that our family photo history really is every bit as important as I thought it was, but he also sparked some new ideas for ways albums can be even more powerful than I'd imagined in raising our kids.

* * *

Nancy: Dr. Condrell, I know how important photo albums were to me as I grew up. And I know I'm not alone in that. Why do kids have that special connection?

Dr. Condrell: In my experience, when parents spend fun and loving time with their children, the children feel valued, desired and special. These feelings pump up a child's self-esteem. And sharing family photos of special times together is one of the best ways I know to do that.

It's really a unique experience – they are doing with you what they can't do with anyone else. Board games, card games, puzzles... They can play those with anyone. But playing with family photos and photo albums is something they only do with Mom and Dad.

And here's another point. Photos tell the real-life stories of your children. Children love stories. So using photos is a wonderful way to grab their attention – to help them learn about relatives that maybe they have yet to meet and the values and traditions your family cherishes.

Actually, I think photos and scrapbooks might be a parent's secret weapon. There are few tools out there that are more powerful or effective in helping to raise confident, happy, well-adjusted kids.

Nancy: Wow, that's a strong statement.

Dr. Condrell: It is, but I totally believe it to be true. You see, whether it's in a scrapbook or on the wall or on the refrigerator, a photo speaks volumes to children each time it catches their eyes. The photo says, "Hey, somebody thought what I did that day was really special," or, "Here I am, surrounded by all my friends."

This is the key point: Keeping photographs around the house is a form of validation for children. It lets them know they matter and they are loved, and these are the kinds of feelings that empower them to feel confident and self-assured. And it doesn't require any special training or fancy education on your part. Anyone can provide this amazing benefit to their children with just photos and words.

Nancy: I guess I always knew that in my heart, but what is the science behind it?

Dr. Condrell: It ties into a concept in child psychology called individuation. Essentially, what that means is that a child begins life feeling as if they're totally welded to their parents. They don't see themselves as individuals. Not at all.

But as you're showing them photographs and as they're identifying themselves in relation to their brothers and sisters and their cousins and grandparents, they develop a sense that they *are* individuals and that they *are* their own people. This is when they begin to use the word "I" and they realize they can suddenly do a lot of things on their own. (At the same time, those family photos are reinforcing their sense that they are surrounded by this family safety net, so they feel secure and loved and able to try new things.)

We as parents oftentimes take that growth stage for granted, but it's so important. And photographs can play a major part. With individuation comes a feeling of independence and competence to do things on our own.

Nancy: My daughter Ashby is 3, and she gets so excited whenever I bring out our photos and albums. Is that because young children are just naturally more visual?

Dr. Condrell: Well, that's certainly part of it. Young children are very concrete; and by that I mean that they examine their world – their environment – by looking at it, tasting it, touching it, smelling it and playing with it. Their senses are everything. They don't think in the abstract.

Here's an example. When my granddaughter was about 3½ she was bragging about how she knew her ABCs. (Never mind that she never made it past G. She was learning and proud of it!) One time I teasingly prompted her, "I'll bet you can't say that backwards." And of course she did – she turned around so her back was to me and she recited, "A-B-C-D-E-F-G." So we've got to remember how kids' minds work at that age and how they take in information.

And also think about this. When you sit down with Ashby and the two of you are looking at photographs or pages in a scrapbook and you're telling her stories about the people in them, what are you doing? She's probably in your lap or your arm is around her. You're in some sort of a loving context. That feeling of love carries over to those pictures and the memories she will always have about them.

Photos are proof to children that they are loved. I've learned from counseling thousands of children over the years that sitting down over family photo-

graphs is one of the best ways to show them the special place they hold in your heart. And that gives them confidence and a sense of self-worth, which are critical to development.

Nancy: Oh, I agree. But recently I read that children don't really begin to recognize people in photographs until they're about 1 year old, and I've been showing Ashby photos of herself ever since she could open her eyes. My instincts just tell me it's very important. Am I correct?

Dr. Condrell: Yes, you are. You know, we don't wait until our children can read before we start telling them bedtime stories. It's the same with photographs. We don't have to wait till our children understand what pictures are and how they're made before we start talking to them about pictures.

I've often felt what a shame it is that children can't remember the first couple years of their lives. Because if they come into a truly loving family, there are so many wonderful things going on all around them – and they have no memory of them.

That, of course, is where photos come in. You can point to a picture and say, "See how you looked when you came home from the hospital? See how happy Grandma was to be holding you?"

Nancy: And, really, photos can help you fill in the years at any point in your life. It was shoeboxes full of photos that helped me get to know my two incredible stepsons, Tyler and Carson, who were already 8 and 5 years old when they came into my life. One of the first things I did was to make albums for each of them. They couldn't stop telling me the stories behind all the pictures, and I could tell the albums really made them feel like important people in my life because I took the time to document their lives. To this day, they still bring me their A+ papers and drawings, "for the scrapbook!"

Dr. Condrell: Nancy, that's wonderful. Stepfamilies and blended families are probably the most complex family structures in the world, and unfortunately, those families struggle because there are so many unspoken or unresolved expectations and fears – both on the part of the children and their new parents. Spending private time with new stepchildren is so important to forming a blended family, and so making those albums was the perfect thing to do.

Nancy: That experience showed me all over again the power that albums can have, and I began to wonder about other ways I could use them. You know, moms today want to instill so many important traditions and values in their kids – everything from being kind to the planet to eating healthier. Is there a way albums can help us do things like that?

Dr. Condrell: Oh, definitely. In my practice, I'm continually amazed by the power of photos to heal and to change. So why couldn't a scrapbook album have the same effect – especially one you put together with a specific goal in mind?

You used the example of teaching kids to be kind to the planet and live greener. Well, if you really want to get kids to value everything that's living, you talk to them about these things. And maybe you make a project out of something like putting out bird feeders, and then you photograph what you're doing for your album and let your kids write about why it's so important.

Nancy: To introduce Ashby to Earth Day, I've been thinking about letting her get all dirty in the yard while we help her plant a tree. The photos we take that day would be just the start. Then we could take more each season or each year to show how much everything – and everyone – has grown.

Dr. Condrell: Exactly. And that taps into something else that's so important to kids. One of the reasons kids love to look at themselves in photos – and especially when those photos are arranged in sequence as they might be in an album – is that the photos give them proof that they're growing up. They can see the physical changes from year to year. And every kid wants to be grown up.

Nancy: Lately I've been tossing around ways I could use my albums to raise a healthier family. Or do you think that's too much of a stretch?

Dr. Condrell: I don't think that's a stretch at all – as long as you approach it in a positive way. And by that I mean you could do something like teaching kids to grow vegetables – to have their own garden so they get introduced to a variety of foods that many of them have never really explored before.

But you photograph the planting, the growing, the harvesting and especially the eating, and you put all that in your album. I think kids are more likely to try food that they've personally grown than something they just got from the supermarket.

Nancy: I can already picture what a great album that would make! For kids, taking care of their garden – the watering and the weeding – could be almost like taking care of a pet. And then, of course, we'd have to do a family recipe album showing us cooking up everything we've grown!

Dr. Condrell: Absolutely. Even for preschoolers, planting seeds, photographing the process and the harvest – those photos and memories can be a foundation for a lifetime of eating healthy. But be prepared to make it fun.

When my granddaughter was younger, I suggested that we plant some seeds and grow vegetables, and this was the reaction I got: "Grampa, watching plants grow is boring!" And of course she's right. But when you take pictures of your garden as it's growing and you put them in a scrapbook, they get to see it all in time-lapse photography. Kids are fascinated by that. It's like they're watching the garden grow right before their eyes.

*   *   *

DR. CONDRELL AND I didn't talk just about the ways family photos and scrapbook albums enrich kids' lives. Their magic doesn't stop when you become an adult. I know for a fact that my family's photo history is as important to me today as it ever was.

And I know it's the same for Dr. Condrell. We even talked about the "wedding wall" his wife Barbara has created in their home. The picture of their own wedding is there – and so are pictures of their parents getting married and their children when they walked down the aisle.

"When you have these up on the wall," he told me, "there's a certain closeness, a certain satisfaction you feel as you walk by. Even if it's just a glance."

And he also left me with this thought....

There's never been a time in history when so many millions of people have owned a camera – even if it's just a camera in their phone. This is a wonderful time we're in. But as easy as it is for us to take pictures now, I hope we don't take them for granted. I hope we don't forget about the power and the significance they have in our lives.

All that growing up and all those good times that Mom captured meant Karen and I always knew how loved and special we were.

NOTE: See the fading and yellowing on some of these old (well, not THAT old) photos? Oh how I wish the photo-safe products that are available now were available to Mom back then. (Check out page 72.)

Nancy Humphries has been named Coastal Academy's "Miss Retrospect" and Missy McDuffie "Miss Junior Retrospect."

Miss Humphries, a senior, is treasurer of the Beta Club and treasurer of the Spanish Club. She is a member of the Civinettes, the Math Team and the varsity basketball and volleyball teams. Her hobbies are playing tennis, going to the beach and water skiing.

The winners were crowned by outgoing queens Mary Anna Pinner, "Miss Retrospect," and Mary Louise Ramsdale, "Miss Junior Retrospect."

The 53 contestants were judged on poise and beauty and wore evening gowns for the pageant. There was no talent competition.

The pageant was open to any girl in grades 7-12. Contestants were sponsored by local businesses.

The title is derived from the name of Coastal Academy's yearbook, the Retrospect.

Nancy Humphries

Academy beauty wins title

The SUN NEWS, Myrtle Beach, S.C., Wednesday, November 24, 1982

GREAT STORIES
They Start With Great Questions

"I find that most people know what a story is until they sit down to write one."

—Flannery O'Connor

IF THERE'S ONE THING I'VE LEARNED in my career it's that, at the end of the day, it all comes down to the story.

When you're a reporter, you're telling other people's stories. You're doing it in a way that honors those stories and, at the same time, makes them compelling for somebody who's hearing them for the first time. That was true when I started as a local cub reporter at WPDE-TV in Florence-Myrtle Beach, South Carolina, and it was true when I co-hosted *Access Hollywood* for a national audience.

I've been privileged to interview a lot of A-list celebrities on the red carpet. I feel even more privileged to write about lots of priceless family stories on the pages of my scrapbooks. And you know what? I don't think the two are all that different. In fact, I've always thought of interviewing as just another form of storytelling. It's storytelling you have to do on the spot.

Getting a great interview and telling a great story both depend on asking the right questions. Now, I know what you're thinking: *I'm sitting here at my table, journaling on an album page. I'm not out doing an interview.*

Well, you really are – sort of.

You see, every time you sit down to write, whether you realize it or not, you're interviewing yourself about the story you want to tell and the best way to tell it. It may be totally subconscious, but you're asking yourself a ton of questions.

What's the one message I want to get across here? And why is it so important to me? What details do I absolutely, positively have to include? Which ones should I leave out?

And maybe most important of all ...

How does writing about this make me feel? And how can I put that into words? When people read what I've written, how do I hope it will make them feel?

So I'm convinced it really does all come down to the questions we ask. And since I've had more than a little experience asking questions, let me share some of the interviewing/storytelling tips that have worked so well for me on the red carpet ... and on the beige carpet. (That's the one at home where I spread out all my scrapping stuff!)

* * *

Be curious. I know I just said that the best stories start with the best questions, but sometimes they start simply because you had the guts to ask a question in the first place. That's what happened when I asked Jack Nicholson how he got started wearing his trademark sunglasses. It sounds like such a simple question, but I was honestly curious. And I thought if I was curious, then lots of other folks might be too.

Now, Jack Nicholson is famous for a lot of things, and one of them is that he does not do interviews. But in 1998, the iconic actor was receiving the prestigious Jack Webb Award from the Los Angeles Police Department. And I was there for *Access Hollywood*. This was fairly early in my *Access* career, so when my producer told me to try and get a Jack Nicholson interview, I thought he had to be joking.

Once I was there though, I figured I might as well give it a try. What did I have to lose? So I simply walked up to him and started asking questions. And

Don't just assume you know all the answers. If there's something you wonder, ask the question! Ask it directly but with love and respect. The answers may surprise you. And when they do, they'll make that album page – and that memory – so much better! It did in the case of this interview with the legendary Jack Nicholson.

you know what? He started answering them. He was so charming and, to everyone's surprise, it turned into a wonderful, 25-minute interview. And then I got around to the sunglasses.

Like a lot of people, I always thought he wore them just because they look so cool on him. (Because he *is* so cool!) Turns out I couldn't have been more wrong! What he told me was that, since he's photographed so often at all the events he goes to, the flashbulbs began to hurt his eyes. And he only wears those shades for protection. Makes total sense!

Well, my producer was giddy that I got the interview in the first place. But he was especially excited that I went out on a limb and asked about the sunglasses. It seemed like such an obvious question, but it sure didn't get the obvious answer. And I think Jack appreciated it too. I remember his reaction almost seemed to say: *Well I'm glad somebody finally got THAT one out there!*

Be curious. Ask a few good questions and you can turn a page of simple soccer pictures into a story you'll look back on and smile years from now.

When it comes to your photos and albums, this means gently and lovingly asking the questions you might not think of asking at first glance. Things like, "Sweetie, why were you making that face?" Or, "What made you decide to wear the bear costume?" Or, "What did you do while you waited for your hair to grow back?"

If there's a moral here, it's simply this: When you sit down to journal on an album page and you get this vague feeling that there's more to this story that *you* want to know, trust your instincts. Try and find it. Don't be afraid to ask questions. Because the people who see your album? They're gonna want to know it too.

Tell the backstory. Hollywood is full of backstories. When Mickey Rourke snagged all those Best Actor nominations in 2009 for *The Wrestler*, everybody agreed he deserved them. But what we all found just as fascinating was the backstory of how that comeback role paralleled the comeback he'd made in real life.

Tell the backstory. They say a picture's worth a thousand words, but sometimes just the opposite is true. Sometimes you need a few words to set up the photo so the whole page pays off.

It's the same with the photos on your album pages. Ask yourself if what led up to a photo – or what happened seconds after you took it – might be more interesting than what's in the picture itself. If the answer is yes, then make that backstory what you write about.

That was sure the case when my mom posed for the picture below, outside the house she grew up in as a little girl in Union, South Carolina. It turns out the house was steeped in history. It was once owned by General William H. Wallace, who was visited by Jefferson Davis, President of the Confederacy, in

1865 – just as Robert E. Lee was surrendering. So in 1938, a marker was erected in front of the house to commemorate the history of that visit, and my mom was the little girl who was chosen to unveil it.

Now, Mom was only 5 at the time. And she didn't really want any part of it. At that age, I'm sure she couldn't have cared less about the doggone marker or the history behind it! But her aunt got her to cooperate with the photographer by telling her that if she would just lift up the sheet ... she'd find a bunch of candy underneath.

So Mom excitedly played her part. And, of course, she was shattered when all she found underneath was that old monument!

This picture's cute on its own. But the stone-cold reality of candyless disappointment makes the backstory so much more poignant!

Fortunately, my grandmother, being the great mom she was, immediately took Mom out to get some candy, just as she'd been promised.

It wasn't until decades later that Mom finally got around to telling me the story behind that picture. And that added even more to the story. Because even though we laughed loudly about it, after all those years I could still hear a little trace in her voice of the bittersweet disappointment she felt that day.

Take journaling shortcuts. I like to journal on my album pages. I like it a lot! (It's just the reporter in me.) But I know there's a limit to the number of words I can cram on a page, no matter how big it is or how tiny I'm able to write. So I find ways to help me say all the things I want to say ... without actually having to say them all.

Let me show you what I mean. When I was growing up, Mom drove me to all my middle school and high school basketball games. And we were always on the road in the winter at holiday time. Without fail, we'd find ourselves listening to this cassette Mom had of Kenny Rogers' *Christmas* album. We knew every word to every song by heart, and sometimes we'd sing them together.

A newspaper article is a great shortcut to capture the facts. Basketball was my favorite sport growing up, and this album full of clippings about my team was the first I made on my own as a kid!

Even after I'd graduated college, whenever I'd play that tape, Mom and I would both start to get a little misty as soon as we'd hear the first few words.

For us, that record became a touchstone; a kind of memory shorthand. When I go back and look at the scrapbook pages Mom made about my basketball years, all I have to see is the words "Kenny Rogers" in her journaling and suddenly I'm right back in that car with her, headed off to a game and hearing those songs again.

Everybody has their own personal touchstones, and music just happens to be one of mine. So now, whether it's a piece of sheet music or a song lyric or a concert ticket or a CD cover, I look for ways to add those cues to my pages. There's no quicker way for me to set the stage for the time or the place or the mood about which I want to write. You can accomplish this same kind of connection with a famous quote or a line from a favorite movie or TV show. Or you can just write light by using things like lists or bullet points to help you save some time and space. You can also use memorabilia like newspaper clippings or brochures to cover the facts and let you get right to the heart!

Do your homework. I'll be the first to admit it – I like to be über-prepared when I step out onto the red carpet. I mean, I want to know everybody who's nominated, everybody who's presenting and friggin' everything that's been written about them in the press! And if I'm lucky, my research will turn up the one tidbit of information that prompts the right question that makes for a super interview.

That's exactly what happened when I was reading up on Johnny Depp. I saw that he'd credited his daughter, Lily-Rose Melody, for the amazing voice he gave his Willy Wonka character in *Charlie and the Chocolate Factory*. I was so intrigued, but that was all I could find out. I was hosting NBC's live red carpet arrival show for the 2005 Golden Globes, where he was nominated for Best Actor, and I hoped I'd have the chance to get the whole story.

Well I got my wish. He told me he'd come up with a number of different voices for Willy Wonka but couldn't decide which one worked. Then he tried them all out on his daughter to get her reaction. She became his personal laugh-o-meter! The voice that made her laugh the hardest? That's the one he gave Willy Wonka.

That one tiny detail ended up making our interview so special, and it's the same when I sit down to journal. I'm not saying you need to turn telling your story into a homework assignment, but here's a little tip that works for me when I'm looking for those make-it-or-break-it details:

When I want to write about a photo and there are things I just can't remember about it – maybe it's really old or I've just forgotten – I'll e-mail it to my dad or my sister or my friends and ask them what they remember about it.

In fact, even when you do remember the details yourself, asking different friends and family members to share their recollections about a photo can

Do your homework. Tell the story as you remember it. But don't stop there. Ask others for their input. Not only will they help make sure you don't miss anything, they'll also help you create a rich, multi-faceted story.

really jump-start your journaling. (Asking kids what's going on in a photo – whether they really know or not – can get some totally entertaining results.) It's like the telephone game you played as a kid – nobody will tell you exactly the same thing. Suddenly your single-focus perspective on that person or that event gets replaced by a 360-degree view and you're finding out all kinds of new things.

Put yourself in the picture. When we write about our kids, it's natural for us to want to make them the stars of our stories. We can't say enough about what they did, what they wore, that last crazy thing they said…. Now, for heaven's sake, don't stop doing that. But do remember to put yourself in the story.

Ask yourself: *How did I feel about this event or this moment? What was going through my mind the second I clicked the shutter? What do I wish I had said then that I can write about now?* Then include all that in your journaling.

Put yourself in the picture. Go beyond who, what, when and where to explain how those photos and the moments they capture made you feel. This is one big chance for your kids to look back and feel your love and validation.

The photos and program you saved from your son's graduation ceremony – of course they'll mean tons to him when he looks back on them years from now. But it's you opening up on the page about what was in your heart that he won't get anywhere else. Don't hesitate to share your feelings and emotions. It's a gift no one but you can give.

Someday Ashby will get that gift when she goes back and reads all about how her mom goofed on the day of her third birthday party. You see, Ashby absolutely loves *The Little Mermaid,* and I was so excited because I was going to surprise her by having Ariel make a personal appearance at her party! (Well, an actress I'd hired who'd be dressed as Ariel, anyway.)

So this lovely woman arrived in her shimmering mermaid outfit and her brilliant, red wig, and Ashby took one look and was beyond excited. I actually don't know who was more excited because I'd spent so much time anticipating and imagining this moment in my mind.

It was a beautiful moment of pure and glorious childhood glee ... until Ashby grabbed Ariel's hand and said, "Let's go swimming together!"

Just look at Ashby's face when Ariel told her she wasn't going swimming. And, of course, there's the corresponding, "Oops! I didn't think of that" look on my face!

Of course, the last thing that costume was designed for was swimming. So the actress stammered something about how she's sorry but she can't go swimming today. With our pool just a few feet away from them in the backyard, that story wasn't adding up for Ashby. She was practically heartbroken: *What do you mean, you can't go swimming? You're a mermaid. You're Ariel. It's what you do!*

Why, oh why it never dawned on me that Ashby would naturally expect to swim with Ariel, I will never know. But when my birthday surprise took that left turn, I do know my excitement became tinged with guilt. In spite of my best intentions, I'd somehow managed to disappoint my precious baby girl.

I could tell right then and there that this was something I needed to journal about. I'd have tons of photos to remind me of all the things that happened that day, but journaling would be my only record of the way I felt.

Well, I did journal about the birthday party with the landlocked mermaid and how, for a little while, I felt I'd made the dumbest mistake of my whole life. And you know what? By the time I was done, I could laugh about the whole thing and see it for the crazy keepsake family moment it was.

Someday, in some way, I know the words I wrote that day will bring Ashby a laugh as well. And maybe they'll even help her through a tempest in a teacup as she's raising a daughter of her own!

*   *   *

THIS LAST TIP won't necessarily help you tell a better story. But I guarantee it will make the stories you do tell so much better. Let me explain.

When Mom passed, one of the albums that Dad had stored away and sent to me was my mom's baby book – the scrapbook Grandmama made for my mom back in the 1930s when Mom was just a baby. As I opened it, it wasn't the wonderful pictures that started me crying. It was Grandmama's *handwriting*.

That was all it took to open a floodgate of memories. I remembered sitting at Grandmama's table as a little girl and looking up at the grocery lists she would put around her kitchen and thinking she had the most beautiful handwriting in the whole wide world. Then I remembered her letters. Even when she was in her 80s and 90s, she would send me these long, carefully handwritten letters full of reminiscences about our times together. I saved every one.

Your handwriting – it's as personal as your smile or the sound of your voice. And it belongs on your album pages. When you read computer journaling, the words are there, alright. It's just that some of the "you" is missing. Now, having said that, I'll also tell you that I love to journal on my computer as much as anybody. Everything comes out all neat and lined up. It fixes the words I still can't seem to spell. But there are times I stop myself from putting that printout on my album page. Instead I make it my script for a version I write by hand. To me, that's the best of both worlds.

And please – no excuses about how *My handwriting is too sloppy* or *I'm afraid I'll make a mistake and mess up this beautiful page I made.* I've never seen your handwriting, but I can tell you right now it's gorgeous. *Because it's your own.*

If you're worried about making a mistake and having to cross something out right as you get to the last line, there's a cure for that too. Make a mistake on the first line and cross it out. Now you can stop your worrying!

The baby book Grandmama made for Mom was full of those so-called mistakes, where the words didn't always stay between the lines. And it's funny, but I think I treasure them more than the words that did stay between the lines.

All I know is, I'm thankful Grandmama never had a computer!

> Baby's First Step
> Betty walked a step or two of her own accord on her first birthday. She had walked a little previously – with assistance. Thereafter, she learned quickly and was soon toddling wherever she liked about the house.

Reading Grandmama's handwritten words somehow feels a little like she's here with me. And thanks to her journaling, I discovered that Ashby and my mother hit the walking milestone at the same time – on their first birthday … how cool!

BETTER PICTURES
They're Easier Than You Think

*My great friend Ulrica is a talented writer and a wonderful photographer.
She's always been so generous in sharing her amazingly easy photo-taking
tips with me. Now she gets to share them with you!*

> *"There are no rules for good photographs,*
> *there are only good photographs."*
> —*Ansel Adams*

NOBODY I KNOW photographs kids quite like my dear friend, Ulrica Wihlborg. Besides being an assistant editor at *People* magazine, she's also a professional lifestyle photographer. Talk about multitalented!

Although I first met her when she covered my wedding for *People,* it was after Ashby was born and we started sharing stories and photos of our little ones that our friendship really started to click.

Nancy: I remember the Christmas card you sent my family. I was completely captivated by the picture of your son, Axel, on it. He was on an antique tractor that was sitting on a dirt road, and I thought it was the cutest photograph of a little boy I'd ever seen. I had to know the name of that photographer so I could arrange a shoot with Ashby. At the time, I only knew you as an editor at *People*. I had no idea you were the photographer! What was the inspiration behind that photo?

Ulrica: I took that photo in Sweden in 2008. The tractor was sitting by the side of the road, and it just caught my eye. Axel was only a year and a half old, and he obviously thought it was cool! He just looks so happy. I take millions of photographs of my kids, and this one of him smiling turned out really genuine and natural.

I think I chose the tractor because, growing up in Sweden, I was around a lot of vintage things that were old and rusty and said "country." They have a timeless look that's something I like to bring to my photographs.

Nancy: I'm sure it's partly because of your editorial background and the way you're able to capture stories with words, but your pictures have this remarkable way of telling a story all on their own. How do you manage that?

Ulrica: Well, I think you have to try to go beyond the obvious shots of people smiling at the camera and saying, "Hi, here I am!" I like to look for all of the other little details I can photograph that will remind me why that moment was so special.

Your daughter's first day at school – of course you have a picture of hugging her as you drop her off in front of the building. But then also turn her around and take a close-in photo of just her backpack. Take a photo of the shoes she's wearing, all tied up and perfect. And take a photo of the sign with the school's name, too, to complete your story.

It's amazing how, together, these little things will trigger memories in years to come. The photos become much more than just pictures of a backpack or a pair of shoes when they bring back memories you'd long forgotten. And that's really what I believe our photos should be about – capturing the memory and not just the moment.

Nancy: I love that idea – capturing the complete memory. It kind of makes you stop and think about all the reasons that memory is so special. Is that the way you see it too?

Ulrica: Exactly. And once you sort of train your eye to take in those details, it becomes almost second nature and you begin to notice more of them. You find yourself saying, *Well, I've got to have a picture of THAT*! It becomes spontaneous.

The other thing that happens, and to me this is the most important, is that it makes you slow down. It counters the temptation to be snap-happy.

Digital photography has so revolutionized the way we take pictures. But with the cameras we have today, it's almost too easy to just shoot, shoot, shoot and hope that one of your photos will turn out.

That's probably the number one mistake I see people make. I believe we need to approach each shot with the idea of making it as good as it can be and not a potential throwaway. We all know we can crop and retouch our images later. But if you try and fool yourself into thinking that you can't, you're going to get a better result to start with.

If we all did only that one thing, we'd instantly be taking better pictures. And we would, no doubt, have lots fewer of them to download to our computer, sort through, back up, print and possibly even make us feel a little overwhelmed when we sit down to turn them into an album!

*   *   *

ULRICA AND I then got down to the real nits and grits. OK, I said. I will slow down the next time I get ready to photograph my kids. I will take an extra second to try and make each shot a keeper. But what exactly can I do better?

Here's what she told me....

Simplify, simplify, simplify. This is probably my Swedish heritage coming through. I like to bring the simplicity and clean lines of Scandinavian design to my photographs. I think it lends a certain keepsake quality when there are just one or two things in a photo that speak to you.

Dark objects in the background can be distracting.   *A clean background keeps the focus on your subject.*

The best way I know of to do that is to de-clutter the background. If you're treating your little one to an impromptu bath in the kitchen sink that you want to capture on film, simply take a moment to move aside some of the things you have on your counter.

Dark objects are always red flags for me – they tend to pop out in the final print almost more than they do in real life, even if they're small. If there's one in my shot and I can't move it out of the way, I'll try to shoot around it by varying the angle or just moving in closer.

Screen the sun. There's a myth that full, unfiltered, midday sun is ideal for taking outdoor photos. But in reality it's often unflattering. If the sun is in front of your subjects, you can end up with squinty-eyed expressions or shadows where you don't want them. If the sun is behind them, it's possible to take a really beautiful shot ... but you would need to meter your camera manually. If you're using a camera with programmed modes, as most people do, that can throw off your metering so your subjects appear as if they're in the dark.

I find open shade the easiest way to get good, even light on your subject. For example, look for a spot that's not directly under a tree but off to the side where there's still shade but nothing hanging right above. I also love shooting kids at sunset for the wonderful warmth that the light has then. It can be a bit yellow, and it just looks beautiful and soft.

Direct sunlight can leave harsh, unflattering shadows.

Open shade gives a more gentle, even effect.

Color-coordinate your shots. This isn't always possible when you're shooting spontaneously, of course. But when you're the one arranging the shot – when you gather the family to take a holiday photo, for instance – you have much more control. You can nix all the loud stripes and the T-shirts with the logos on them in favor of a simple, uniform color palette.

Every Father's Day, I like to stage a photo shoot of my husband and our two sons as part of my husband's Father's Day gift. And that's one opportunity where I can pay attention to color. It doesn't have to be elaborate. I just think in terms of colors that are more muted and natural and that go well with each other.

There are lots of ways you can coordinate a series of photos when you know you'll be using them together in an album. Let's say your little girl is wearing her favorite pink dress. All it will take is a quick trip to her room and you'll find lots of other things you can add to the shots you take of her or showcase in shots of their own. Maybe there's a pink stuffed bunny you could show her holding in cupped hands. Or perhaps there's another dress she loves that has shades of pink in it, and you could shoot it all by itself on its hanger, hooked over a doorknob.

This truly makes for gorgeous layouts in your scrapbooks when several pictures have the same color in them, and you get the added benefit that the objects bring back memories as well.

For the times you only wish you could have worked more with color, simply convert your photos to black and white. That's a wonderful technique for rescuing a shot that is otherwise great, but where the colors conflict or draw attention away from your subject.

Start with your original subject … but don't stop there. If you're shooting your daughter in her newly decorated (or just cleaned!) room, think about some of the other things you can shoot at the same time. They'll add interest and color coordination to your album page layout now. And they'll add little moments of "I remember that!" fun years from now.

Shoot vertically. When I see parents taking pictures of their kids, they almost never flip the camera vertically. I probably shoot 90 percent of my photos vertically. It's a little thing I do, but right away you eliminate background clutter because you get rid of the space on each side of your subject. To me, shooting vertically works better with the way our bodies are shaped. And I think people just look more beautiful that way.

After you've turned your camera vertically, ask your subject to turn slightly to one side. Suddenly they look pounds thinner, and they'll love the photo you've taken of them!

Apply the Rule of Thirds. I've always said that the so-called rules of photography are the first rules you should break. But this one really can help you take better pictures. Think of your image area as being divided into thirds. Whether you're shooting vertically or horizontally, you have a left third, a center third and a right third. Our natural inclination is to put the subject of our shot smack-dab in that center third (below, left). The Rule of Thirds suggests putting the subject off to one side or the other. It's surprising how such a small framing adjustment can do so much to make your pictures more dynamic.

Before

Get in close. Children make for wonderful close-ups. Kids have such beautiful skin and their eyes are so expressive. So getting really close can give you a great photo. Plus, as the photographer, you'd like to engage children in what you're doing. Moving in close gives you a human connection you don't get when you shoot from a distance.

Ideally, your camera will make you move in close. When people ask me to recommend gear for them, I almost always suggest that they start with a basic digital SLR camera body and a single 50mm f/1.4 fixed lens. Because the lens isn't a zoom, you're the one who's got to do the zooming! This lens is also ideal for blurring out cluttered backgrounds, and it lets in a lot of light so you can take pictures in low-light conditions without having to use your flash.

And one other suggestion: While you're there, with your camera inches away from your little boy or little girl, if the moment seems right, ask them to close their eyes for a shot or two. Normally we toss photos that show people with their eyes closed. But it's often very peaceful, very serene. Not every photo we take needs to show a smile.

After

Most of all, be patient. When you photograph young kids, you won't get very far trying to bark orders about where to stand and how to look. And let's face it, nothing is a bigger mood-killer! So do just the opposite.

Sometimes the best pictures happen because you've set the camera aside. Take a break and get down on your kids' level. Play with them, tickle them, tell them stories. Let them show you the absolute best way to make a mud pie. Then when you pick up the camera again, you'll have images to shoot that you couldn't possibly have imagined before.

*   *   *

Nancy: I can't wait to try out those techniques. But I'm gonna play devil's advocate for a second. Some people are bound to be thinking, *That sounds like too much work. I want to relax when I take pictures.* What do you say to folks who say *thinking* about their shots takes away some of the fun?

Ulrica: Oh, but the simple act of thinking about the photo you're going to take makes it *more* fun! It only takes a couple of seconds, but it connects you with your feelings. It keeps you in the moment. It's like anything you do – when you put your best into it, it makes you feel happy. When you care about what you're doing, there's a certain satisfaction you get in knowing that you've done it right.

And you get to see the results on paper every time you print one of your pictures.

Nancy: My red-carpet mentality is showing through here because I usually save my most burning question for last. So here goes: From photographing so many kids and capturing such beautiful images ... what's the biggest secret you've learned for photographing children?

Ulrica: It's not really a secret, but it almost always results in pictures that are more alive and more natural. Simply give your kids something to do.

We're so used to seeing typical studio images where a little girl is wearing a pretty dress and she's sitting in a chair and she's looking straight at the camera. I think some parents try to emulate that photo style when the truth is, they could easily do so much better.

If you remember the first time I came over to photograph Ashby, she was 18 months old. And we both know how impossible it is for little ones to sit still! So I brought along one of those wooden barrels that's been cut in half and we set it up and filled it with water to let her splash around in. Kids love the water, and she was a little trouper for our whole shoot.

But you don't really need props to get interesting shots. Ask a group of kids to lie on the ground next to each other, head to head, and shoot from above so that just their faces fill the frame. It's obviously a very staged pose and not something they're used to doing, and that's why it always starts them giggling. Kids immediately begin to relax when you ask them to get down on the ground, so you're going to get great, happy, genuine smiles.

For older kids, maybe 4 or 5, think of something you can all do together, like making pancakes or decorating muffins or, really, any activity that they enjoy. It makes the photos natural and true to life, and you end up with images that express who they are as human beings.

As a mom, if you were to start a family tradition of photographing that same activity in the same place and the same time – maybe once each month or once each season or once each year – you would have such a priceless document of your child's growth. It can be really fun to style and create your own photo shoot! And at the same time, the two of you would be bonding over something you both enjoy.

Best of all, it would make those photo sessions something she would always cherish and look forward to.

TOOLS AND TECHNIQUES
They Make Beautiful Pages Possible

"Anything you can do needs to be done, so pick up the tool of your choice and get started."

—Ben Linder

I LOVE MY ALBUMS. I love looking through them and sharing them. But I've got to be honest and admit that I have just as much fun playing with my favorite tools and putting together layouts.

The right tools can make scrapbooking less intimidating for some and positively euphoric for others. These are some of the products I've come to rely on – and some simple tips for putting them to good use.

The bare necessities

OK, there is a lot of scrapbooking stuff out there. I mean a lot. So it's totally easy to get distracted, off track and overwhelmed. That's one reason why it's a good idea to hook up with someone like a Creative Memories Consultant who can explain what does what and help you keep things from getting out of hand.

But if your question is, "What do I need to get started?" here's my short list!

Album

Duh. Of course you need an album. But did you know that not all albums are created equal? You have all kinds of choices to make. I like Creative Memories albums because the strap hinges let the album lie flat when it's open so it's easier to work in and easier to enjoy when you're reading it.

I also trust Creative Memories' lifetime guarantee, and I know that the pages are lignin-free, acid-free and buffered.

Whoa, back up! They're what-free and what?

Lignin is a substance that occurs naturally in wood. (Hey, natural's good, right? Not in this case.) It makes paper turn brown and brittle with age. And it does the same thing to your photos. All the paper used in Creative Memories scrapbook pages has had the lignin removed.

Acid is another thing found in most paper that will damage photos and memorabilia. So it's important that you choose pages, papers and decorations that are acid-free. Creative Memories takes that a step further. They "buffer" their pages with an alkaline reserve of at least 2 percent calcium carbonate. It's like a protective shield against acids in the memorabilia you put into your albums and in the greasy fingerprints your pages will accumulate over a lifetime. (Which reminds me – be sure you put clear, plastic, photo-safe page protectors on every finished page!)

Tape Runner

Love this little rolling tape dispenser! The adhesive's safe for your photos and the tool lets you zip out a little strip of double-stick tape wherever you want it.

Scissors and Personal Trimmer

By cutting or "cropping" your photos, you can focus on the important stuff. You'll also leave more room on the page for journaling (or for more photos). There are some great tools out there that will do amazing things. But all it takes to get started is a good, sharp scissors. I'd also suggest picking up a Creative Memories Personal Trimmer (mini paper cutter) because it's inexpensive and it just makes it so easy to make clean, straight cuts.

Pens

Keep in mind that you're counting on your albums to last a lifetime ... and longer! So when you're choosing a pen, pick something that's going to last. The pigment-based ink in Creative Memories pens is fade-resistant (to hold off the harmful effects of light) and bleed-resistant (so it won't smudge, smear and be lost if your album should ever happen to get wet).

Power® Sort Box

I think the first rule of album-making is to understand that you're not going to get all the photos you want preserved into your albums today. That's why I love these tough little photo-safe plastic boxes. They let you get all your photos organized and safely stored until you get a chance to get to them. And the big box is full of smaller compartment boxes that are so convenient to grab and go so you can work on your albums wherever you are, as time allows. (You'd be amazed at what I can get done between takes on the set!)

Not quite necessities ... but awfully nice to have

Journaling cards

Think index cards – only way prettier. They make your words stand out on a page. And they make it easy to journal whenever you happen to find a few minutes. Then you can add them to your album later. (Seeing a pattern here? For "busy" people, taking care of family photos means fitting it into the cracks in your life rather than waiting for that fantastic scrapbooking weekend that never comes.) You can also find fun quotes like the ones shown at left, beautifully preprinted on delicate vellum paper. Maybe one says just what's on your mind!

Pretty papers

This is where working on your albums really starts to get fun. You'll find papers in every color and pattern imaginable. And you'll start cutting them into all kinds of crazy shapes. Once you get going, you'll fold them, tear them, rumple them up.... Just start out slow and be careful what you use. It was important to me that the papers in my Hummingbird Series be acid-free, lignin-free and buffered so your photos will be safe. I also like the fact that the 12x12 sheets fit exactly onto a Creative Memories scrapbook page and the photo mats perfectly mat a standard 4x6 photo. This way you can create some gorgeous pages quickly, with just paper, photos and tape.

Decorative embellishments

Just start with baby steps. Adorable stickers, paper ribbons.... There's so much out there. You could easily spend more time focused on your decorations than you do on your photos and stories. These "beginner basics" will get you started.

BEGINNER BASICS

Get yourself together. First off, get your photos organized (at least a little bit). Gather them all together and group them by date or group them by subject or group them by occasion ... whatever you think will work best for you. (At this point in the game, how you organize is way less important than the mere idea of getting organized.) You'll save yourself a ton of time in the long run.

Give them the slip. If you're more interested in just getting your photos into albums than you are in cutting, cropping, taping and decorating, consider a photo-safe slip-in album like the one shown below. You can be done in minutes by just slipping in your photos and journaling cards.

Go naked! I have to admit, I giggled when I first heard the term "naked pages" used to describe scrapbooks with just pictures and journaling on the page. But it's a great trick for getting things done quickly. After all, the photos and stories are the most important part! I've met some album-makers who swear by this strategy and make the most amazing albums.

Can't someone do it for you?

Actually, yes. When I talk about scrapbooking, one of the most common fears I hear is that it will just take too much time. But all-in-one scrapbooking kits have become beautiful, convenient, quick options. You can get pages that are already designed and waiting for your photos and journaling, and decorations that are already cut and ready to add wherever you want them. Digital scrapbooking options can be even easier. Creative Memories lets you download free software and then add sets of inexpensive (or free!) predesigned digital page templates. You just drag and drop your photos into the templates to create your digital photo book, and you can have it printed and mailed right to your door.

Fill in the blanks. Don't let yourself get paralyzed by fear of the blank page. Books full of page layout ideas to copy are helpful for many scrapbookers (both beginners and veterans). My Hummingbird Series from Creative Memories goes one step easier by including a few plastic Page Planner templates along with a book full of layout ideas on how to use them.

Keep it simple. If you're just getting started making decorative scrapbook pages, try picking something monochromatic. (Build around a color that stands out in your photos. Or make it even easier by going black and white with either your photos or your decorations.) Choose papers with simple, understandable designs rather than intricate, busy patterns. Doing things like this will help your photos stand out and make your choices easier (double whammy!).

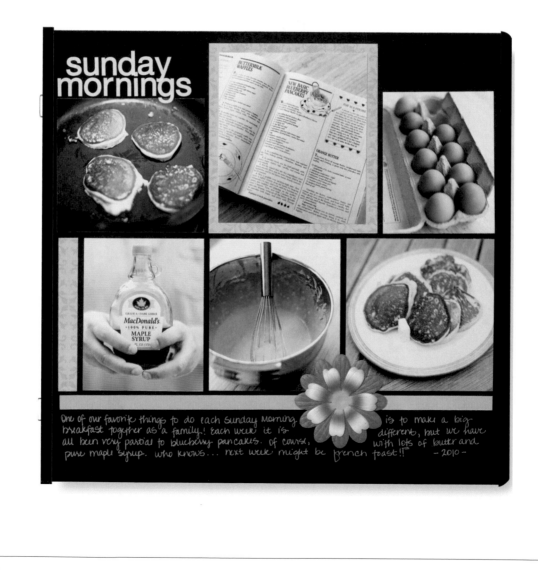

Focus on the photos. Try starting with one photo you really like and emphasizing it by enlarging it or putting a mat behind it. Make this the focal point of your page. Then you could balance that with a cluster of smaller photos on the other side of the page. (And, when you crop your smaller photos, keep it simple at the start. Straight lines are easier to manage than clever crops or shapes.)

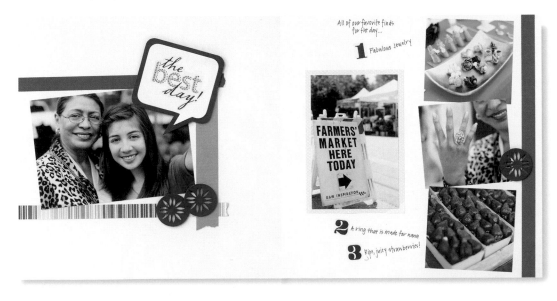

Don't wait for the perfect photo. No matter how many tips my friend Ulrica gives me (check out chapter 4), I may never become a "great" photographer. And that's OK. My albums aren't an art gallery. They're a celebration of the moments in the photos and the memories they contain. So if you don't have one great photo to use as the focal point of your page, try using several pretty good ones! Then you can balance that with a large, colorful die-cut paper shape.

In fact, you might not have any photos at all. You could make a page of just funny quotes from your kids that will become a family favorite.

Journaling is the best decoration. It's your words, your stories and the feelings you get from your photos that make your albums lasting family treasures. In my experience, it's those handwritten notes that carry the most impact. Still, some people let themselves get self-conscious about the way their handwriting looks. And if that's going to stand in your way, by all means, use your computer to type and print your journaling.

A great quote can sometimes get to the heart of what's on your mind quickly. For my Hummingbird Series from Creative Memories, I've picked some personal favorites and we've printed them in fun, beautiful fonts on soft, elegant vellum.

Stack and layer. When you're finally ready to start playing with paper decorations and embellishments, have fun layering things on top of each other. Pick a coordinating set of papers and decorations that will let you experiment without worrying about matching colors.

Tear it up. Rather than spending lots of time precisely measuring and cutting your decorative pieces, try just tearing them. It saves time and gives a fun, informal look. Creative Memories even offers some inexpensive tearing tools to help you rip it just right.

simple pleasures

I really love these carefree days when we have nothing planned but to spend the day together! Our days are so scheduled trying to keep up with our jobs and the boys' activities, these rare moments are extra special.

Lay it down before you tape it down. When you're just beginning, get all your pieces together and play with them on the page like a jigsaw puzzle. Soon you'll start to see shapes and relationships you like. Then you can start taping things into place. (Remember, don't be afraid to use the layout templates I talked about on page 79. It's *much* simpler!)

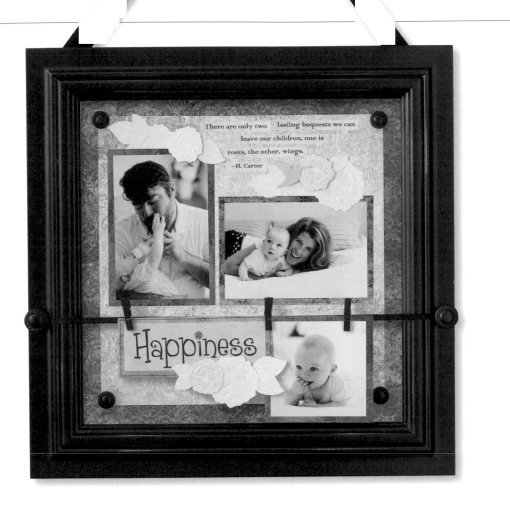

There are only two lasting bequests we can leave our children, one is roots, the other, wings.

—H. Carter

Happiness

Enjoy them every day. In case I've forgotten to mention it, I love my scrapbooks. And some of the pages that end up in my scrapbooks make me happy just looking at them! So it only makes sense to me to put those pages on display and get them into my family's lives. After all, I'm already going to the effort to create the album, right?

One way to do that is with a Magnetic Everyday Display from Creative Memories. It's easy to show off some photos and memorabilia. Or, take a page from your album and put it on display for awhile. Whenever you're ready, you can change your Magnetic Everyday Display and add that page back into the album where it belongs.

*   *   *

That's it. Take your pictures. Tell your stories. Gather your tools and you're ready to roll. So what do you say? Ready to get going? Turn the page and let's start taking a look at all the things we've learned in action!

1ST
BIKE

Enjoy the little things,
for one day you may
look back and realize
they were the big things.

ALBUM PAGE LAYOUTS
Putting it All Together

Baby's Health Record

Betty didn't gain at first— until we realized that she wasn't getting enough to eat. But when we put her on a bottle she gained rapidly and a happier, healthier, baby you never saw.

She has never been sick, except for one or two slight colds and two or three days of flu at fifteen months.

At the age of nineteen and one-half months Betty won a silver cup in a Baby contest for being the healthiest baby in her age group.

Prettiest Baby
Baby Contest
Union, S.C. — June 3, 1935.
Award - silver cup.

"Style is the perfection of a point of view"
—Richard Eberhart

TAKE A LOOK at the pages from my mother's and grandmother's albums (pages 20, 23, 39, 53 and above). Then look at some of the pages from my albums (pages 92-113). Now look at the rest of the layouts in this chapter.

What you show and tell on your photo album pages makes them special. But the way you show and tell makes those pages yours. What I mean by that is no one can teach you how to scrapbook because no one has your heart.

You may choose to start out straight and simple, like my mom, with just pictures and words. Or you might like to begin by simply copying some of the fancier layouts you'll see in this chapter (we've included simple instructions for you online – check out page 166). The point is, no one can ever tell you you've done it wrong. And that's part of the beauty of photo albums. They're part of you … on paper. What's not to love?

BETTY'S BISCUITS. This is one of my favorite double-duty uses for a scrapbook album. It also serves as a keepsake family recipe book. I asked everyone in my family to write down favorite recipes in their own handwriting. Then I added pictures of the cook, the finished dish and the family making that recipe. I think using an album to engage with the kids and prepare family favorites sounds like just what Dr. Condrell suggested!

TIPS Chapter 2—Albums can help raise a healthy family, Chapter 4—Shoot vertically / Get close

PRODUCTS USED Reminisce Autumn Additions, Reminisce Title Stickers, Simply Beautiful Title Stickers, Simply Beautiful Decorative ABC Stickers, Reminisce Paper Flowers, Brick Cardstock Paper

I can't believe my baby girl is 3 already! Mama had planned a small, intimate family party until Ashby came up and said, "Mama, when are all my friends coming over for my BIG Ariel princess party!?" So in a matter of two days, Mama planned everything Ariel! It quickly went from a family party to a party of 60! All worth it as Ashby had a blast playing with all her friends, eating cake and taking photos non-stop (just like Mama). But at the very end of the day, she just wanted to hang with her family.

ASHBY'S 3RD BIRTHDAY was truly one for the books. This layout captures the highlights. (For the lowlights, check out pages 51-52!) I love a lot of what's going on in this layout, but one fundamental step I want to point out is matting the photos. It's so simple to do and adds a ton of impact. Matting is like your first baby step toward decorative layouts. (And, if you're working with standard 4x6 prints, you can get presized mats so you don't even have to cut anything!)

TIPS Chapter 4—Get close / Be patient, Chapter 5—Keep it simple / Focus on the photos / Stack and layer

PRODUCTS USED Simply Beautiful Birthday Additions, Cardstock Paper (Grape, Sea Glass, White), White Swirly Monogram Stickers, Basic Fine-Tip Pen Set, Foam Squares, Custom Cutting System with Circle Patterns

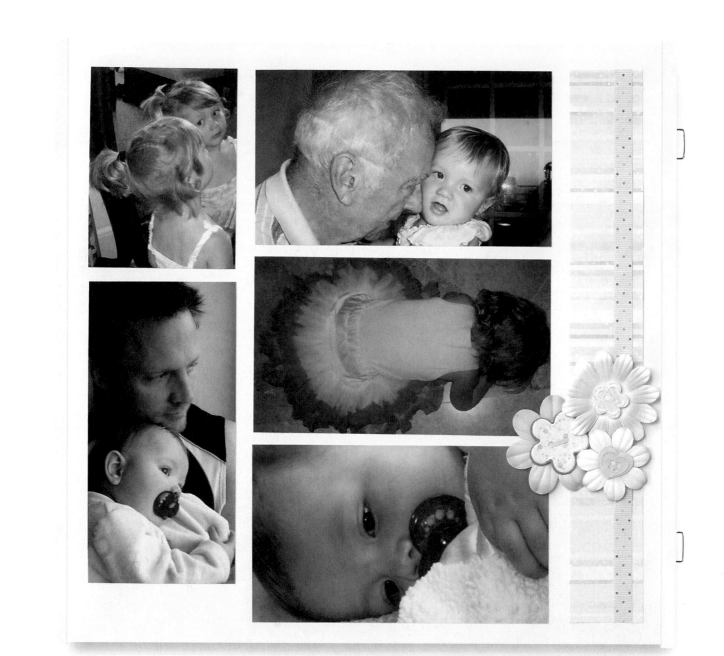

MY ASHBY FAVORITES. These are some of my all-time favorite photos of the most beautiful girl in the world (in my opinion!). And, while I could have created a fancy layout, the old phrase, "gilding the lily" came to mind. So this is pretty much just the photos and words. Easy. But notice how the photos are cropped and lined up, so everything feels evenly spaced. And the super-simple borders on inside edges seem to pull everything together. This makes a great beginner layout.

Ashby, these are some of Mama's favorite photos she snapped of you! You loving your first ponytail! Da loving you! You and Poppy loving the NYC view. You in your dance skirt not loving the fact you couldn't have a soda. And Mama falling in love with your rosy cheeks, her precious bunny & flower!

TIPS Chapter 2—Photos provide validation, Chapter 4—Shoot vertically / Get close, Chapter 5—Focus on the photos

PRODUCTS USED Delight Designer-Print Paper, Delight Paper Ribbon, Delight Paper Buttons, Delight Paper Flowers, White Ruled Paper, Classic Fine-Tip Pen Set, Foam Squares, Hummingbird Page Planner Templates

There is something so special about the beach, its ocean and waves. By seeing how gorgeous nature is, it just makes you know that God is present; that's exactly how we felt when Carson, Ashby, & Tyler were baptized. What a special day it was to have them baptized all together in Mama's hometown of Myrtle Beach, S.C. and by two special pastors, Uncle Kirk and Rev. Timmerman. And I know Grandmama Betty was present via heaven, along with family, friends, and grandparents who were there in person as this is something she wished to happen.

BAPTISM. The beach was such a perfect setting for the kids' baptism. And it was important for me to get that point across in this layout. It's the waves across the bottom that tie it together for me. Remember in chapter 5 when I suggested tearing papers instead of doing lots of fussy measuring? Creative Memories makes a simple, inexpensive little thing called a Wavy Tearing Tool that lets you just rip up a border like this. Love it!

TIPS Chapter 3—Put yourself in the picture, Chapter 4—Simplify / Color-coordinate your shots / Shoot vertically, Chapter 5—Keep it simple / Journaling is the best decoration / Tear it up

PRODUCTS USED Cheerful Tone-on-Tone Paper, White Cardstock Paper, White Ruled Paper, White Simple Monogram Stickers, Basic Fine-Tip Pen Set, Wavy Tearing Tool

you've imagined.
— Henry David Thoreau

Go confidently in the direction of your dreams! Live the life

Graduating middle school! We are so proud of you, Tyler! Ashley was so proud, she kept yelling "Hey Ty, Ty!" during the whole ceremony. Nommy cried because you were just a "little teddy bear" when she met you. And Poppy is so sentimental about the fact you go away to college in 4 years... TOO SOON!

GRADUATION DAY. When Tyler graduated from middle school, we were all so excited. I wanted to make sure this page showed off just how proud his father and I – and his whole family – were. For a boy's graduation page though, most of that has to come in the journaling, rather than a lot of frilly decorations. This layout HAD to be simple. One point worth noticing is the way the one big photo (with its colorful mat) works to balance out the page full of smaller photos.

TIPS Chapter 3—Do your homework, Chapter 5—Keep it simple / Focus on the photos / Journaling is the best decoration

PRODUCTS USED Cheerful Tone-on-Tone Paper, Cheerful Storybox, Cheerful Title Stickers, Cheerful Paper Ribbon, Basic Fine-Tip Pen Set

MDA TELETHON. When my mother was diagnosed with ALS, the Muscular Dystrophy Association was there for her (and me!) every step of the way with support, with answers and with an unwavering drive to find a cure. So now I'm proud and honored to help Jerry Lewis with the annual Labor Day telethon. I love the excitement, the time spent with friends and the chance to help out. But most of all, I love the kids!

After Mom's struggle with ALS, events such as these are near & dear to my heart. Any opportunity I have to spread the word and raise funds to help find new treatments and, eventually a cure, I'm there.

As a bonus, spending time with such wonderful friends, some long-time and some new, was simply amazing!

TIPS Chapter 5—Fill in the blanks

PRODUCTS USED StoryBook Creator Plus Software, Reminisce Digital Power® Palette, Simple Click & Fill Digital Pages, Agency FB and CK Becky (fonts)

A DAY TO REMEMBER. Do you think I could ever forget it? Of course not! But it was such a beautiful, wonderful day and I want to be able to share it forever. Someday Ashby and the boys are going to read the words their father and I spoke. And I hope the words inspire them to keep searching till they find someone they feel just as strongly about!

PART OF OUR WEDDING VOWS SPOKEN ON OUR
WEDDING DAY: JUNE 29, 2005

I had heard of soul mates and I know the definition of one, but I truly didn't understand the meaning until I met you! It seems we were given a meant-to-be moment to meet and set the stage for a special future together. You all have become a part of me I cannot live without. Wherever life takes us, I know we will always get by as long as we go together.

A day to remember

It's said that a person isn't whole until they become a part of something bigger than themselves. With you, I become as whole and as complete as I ever dreamed I could. You are my partner; with you, I can do anything. You are the love of my life; with you, I feel emotions more deeply than I ever imagined possible!

TIPS Chapter 3—Take journaling shortcuts, Chapter 4—Color-coordinate your shots, Chapter 5—Keep it simple / Focus on the photos / Journaling is the best decoration

PRODUCTS USED Hummingbird Paper & Photo Mats, Hummingbird Embellishment Pack, Hummingbird Expressions of Life Vellum Accents, Hummingbird Paper Ribbon, White Cardstock Paper, Bright Fine-Tip Pen Set, Foam Squares, Frosted Photo Splits, Custom Cutting System with Circle Patterns

Richard Gere — Richard, Richard, Richard! I've made it no secret I adore him! (Even my husband says he understands). I've had a crush on him ever since I snuck into "American Gigolo" as a little girl! Will never forget one of the first interviews I had with him. I was so flustered, I couldn't get my words out!

Celine Dion — She's so candid and energetic, it is always a blast to chat with her. Love her husband Rene, too! I've gotten to know them both more closely through the years, and they are so wonderful!

Tom Hanks and Rita Wilson — What do I love most about this couple? Everything! Truly THE most delightful couple in Hollywood. They treat everyone with respect, and they are always smiling!

Garth Brooks and Trisha Yearwood — Two of the most gorgeous voices ever, and two of the most genuine people ever. I'm so glad they are my dear friends! They are not those who just "say" they are friends, they truly are!

FAVORITE CELEBS. In my years in this business I've had the opportunity to interview many different celebrities. Many of them I've gotten to know quite well. Some have become personal friends. Here are some of my favorites (and there are more!) and why. Usually it's because they've managed to stay real, humble and kind, despite all of their success and everything thrown their way! In a layout like this, where you have a lot of photos to fit onto the page, try cropping in close. It not only helps you manage space, it also helps direct the focus where you want it.

Halle — Sometimes you click with people from the very beginning. Halle was one of those people and I love when someone exudes beauty on the inside as much as the outside.

Jewel — There's a positive side to everything. We both had to withdraw from DWTS due to knee injuries, but that is how we became friends and I'm so glad of that. She's so sweet!

Taylor Swift — So young and so talented! I cherish the memories of the two full days I spent with her and her family at the CMA's. Beautiful!

Jamie Foxx — He is soooo talented—a great musician, actor, comedian, and SO NICE! Seeing how sweet he was to my baby girl, playing the harmonica for her, made me love him even more! And, I know if I ever need anything—he'd be there to help. He's that kind of guy!

Madonna — From the first time I interviewed Madonna and time and time again after, I was always so impressed. She is intelligent, real, and I love talking to her as a fellow mom.

Chris Daughtry — Fellow southerner! To be a rocker and to be so genuinely kind—he's got it all!

SOMEfavorite celebs

TIPS Chapter 5—Can't someone do it for you? / Focus on the photos

PRODUCTS USED StoryBook Creator Plus Software, Simple Click & Fill Digital Pages, Hummingbird Digital Kit, Simple Digital Alpha Set

DANCING WITH THE STARS

What a thrill to be selected as part of the cast for Dancing With the Stars! Wow. It was such hard work. I will always carry a special respect for professional dancers and the dedication it takes for them to be so good.

Tony Dovolani was an amazing partner, and taught me so much. After three and a half weeks of intense rehearsals, I had the waltz down pat. (I'll bet I could still do that one!)

That's why it was just so frustrating when I tore up my knee (shredded the meniscus) and had to withdraw. I was so disappointed. I just would have loved to have the chance to try. In fact, to this day, whenever I hear Moon River (the song to which we were to dance), I start waltzing!

DWTS! ABC's *Dancing With the Stars* is one of my favorite shows. So I was totally honored to be selected and really looking forward to competing. When I injured my knee and had to drop out, I had so many feelings and memories I wanted to express and capture. Of course they ended up in my albums. Remember, your albums can do more than validate your children – they can recognize your own triumphs and struggles!

So how wonderful is it that such disappointment comes with a great silver lining?
Jewel was also part of the cast that year and injured her knee too.
So even though we were both completely let down about missing out,
we got the chance to get to know each other and become great friends.
It's a friendship I treasure!

TIPS Chapter 4—Color-coordinate your shots / Shoot vertically, Chapter 5—Keep it simple

PRODUCTS USED StoryBook Creator Plus Software, Dress It Up Digital Embellishments, Cheerful Digital Overlays, Archer Medium and Pea Allison (fonts)

live, LOVE, laugh

If I could, I'd protect you
From the sadness in your eyes
Give you courage in a world of compromise
Yes, I would

If I could, I would teach you
All the things I've never learned
And I'd help you cross the bridges that I've burned
Yes, I would

If I could, I would try to shield
Your innocence from time
But a part of life I gave you isn't mine
I've watched you grow, so I could let you go

LIVE, LOVE, LAUGH. Celine Dion's *Miracle* CD had a real impact on me when I was pregnant. (Especially *If I Could*!) The memory of how often I listened to those songs and the way they made me feel is something I definitely wanted to capture in my albums. Now Celine is pregnant and I'm so happy for her. I love that she and Rene shared these family photos, since that CD has forever made Celine an icon of motherhood to me!

If I could, I would help you
Make it through the hungry years
But I know that I can never cry your tears
But I would, if I could

If I live in a time and place where you don't want to be
You don't have to walk along this road with me
My yesterday won't have to be your way

If I knew, I would try to change
The world I brought to you to
And there isn't very much that I, I could do
But I would, if I could

Oh baby, mummy wants to protect you
And help my baby through the hungry years
It's part of

And if you ever, ever need
Sad shoulder to cry on
I'm just someone to talk to
I'll be there, I'll be there

I didn't change your world
But I would, if I could

Oh darling, I love you baby

TIPS Chapter 3—Take journaling shortcuts, Chapter 4—Simplify, Chapter 5— Focus on the photos

PRODUCTS USED StoryBook Creator Plus Software, Nature's Whisper Digital Kit, Distressed Digital Overlays, Worstveld Sling (font)

FRIENDS. You can never have too many friends. I never want to forget any of mine or any of the good times we've had. So a layout like this calls for lots of photos. One of my favorite things about scrapbooking digitally is that you can control the size of your photos. Create lots of small spaces for photos and fill each one with just the focal point of the photo.

The more you **PRAISE** and **celebrate** your life, the more there is in *life* to celebrate.

— OPRAH WINFREY

TIPS Chapter 5—Focus on the photos

PRODUCTS USED StoryBook Creator Plus Software, Hummingbird Digital Kit

A DAY IN THE SUN. This layout does such a wonderful job of getting across a lot of what made the day great. And it does that by using tons of photos! Look at the five small photos across the bottom on the left-hand page. Each of those is part of a bigger photo. But by cropping in tight on the really interesting elements, you can fit more on the page.

TIPS Chapter 3—Use journaling shortcuts, Chapter 5—Don't wait for the perfect photo / Tear it up

PRODUCTS USED Discover Tone-on-Tone Paper, Discover Designer-Print Paper, Discover Paper Ribbon, Discover Paper Buttons, White Cardstock Paper, White Ruled Paper, Brown Sophisticate ABC/123 Stickers, Tearing Tool, Custom Cutting System with Circle Patterns, 12-inch Rotary Trimmer with Deckle Blade, Friendship Micro Maker

simple **PLEASURES**

Ashley and Paul love to go visit their grandparents on the farm. No TV, No Video Games — just animals and tractors... and a whole lot of TLC from Nana and Papa. They come home very tired, but on cloud nine.

Visiting the

VISITING THE FARM. Remember in chapter 4 when Ulrica talked about the great looks you can get when you color-coordinate your photo shoots? This is a great example of what to do when you want to do that, but you're not able to control your whole environment or change everyone's clothes. Shoot in black and white or sepia tones. (Or just change the photos afterward on your computer.) These sepia photos look amazing alongside the jewel-toned papers and decorations.

TIPS Chapter 3—Use your handwriting, Chapter 4—Color-coordinate your shots / Get close

PRODUCTS USED Reminisce Tone-on-Tone Paper, Reminisce Title Stickers, Reminisce Paper Ribbon, Reminisce Paper Flowers, Reminisce Paper Frames, Spargo Ruled Paper, Clay Cardstock Paper, Brown Sophisticate ABC/123 Stickers

Favorites when
you were little...
ferris wheel
cotton candy
balloons and
rides...

FOR YOUR AMUSEMENT. Keep it simple when you're decorating a page. Sometimes that means building around a single color that stands out in your photos. But if your setting is a brilliantly bright, primary colored amusement park, there's a whole palette of colors with which you can safely play!

TIPS Chapter 3—Take journaling shortcuts / Use your handwriting, Chapter 5—Keep it simple

PRODUCTS USED Cheerful Tone-on-Tone Paper, Cardstock Paper (Clay, White), Basic Fine-Tip Pen Set, Custom Cutting System with Circle Patterns, Corner Maker

FOURTH OF JULY. Albums are perfect for capturing the sights of a holiday. But Independence Day is as much about the sounds as it is the sights. That's why I love the backstory on this page that will forever remind this family how ... um ... delightfully annoying those noisemakers were! I also love the way the giant 10x8 photo on the left is balanced out by a whole bunch of photos on the right.

CELEBRATE THIS DAY

WHOSE crazy idea was it to give those kids noise makers? While they had great fun blowing them, my ears hurt! Despite all the noise, it turned out to be a wonderful day — spending it with my sisters and brothers and their families. Maybe next year we will forget the noise makers at home! But still bring the kids. ☺

memories.reminisce.time

TIPS Chapter 3—Tell the backstory, Chapter 4—Look for little details, Chapter 5—Focus on the photos

PRODUCTS USED Reminisce Tone-on-Tone Paper, Reminisce Designer-Print Paper, Reminisce Title Stickers, Reminisce Paper Ribbon, Gray Cardstock Paper, Spargo Ruled Paper, White Sophisticate ABC/123 Stickers, Classic Fine-Tip Pen Set, Foam Squares, 12-inch Rotary Trimmer with Small Wavy Blade, Embossed Star Maker, Galaxy Micro Maker

HEAVEN ON EARTH. The colors in this layout blend together so seamlessly because it lifts a prominent color from the photos (in this case, Dad's shirt), then matches and complements that in the paper choices. Another simple little trick that gives this layout some dimension is the way that some of the papers have been crumpled up and then flattened back out. I love the way that adds some shadows and makes them literally pop off the page!

Our sweet little Sammy, every day you bring us more joy than the day before! You are the perfect baby; so happy and content. You sleep through the night ~ most nights, which is an extra blessing! We waited and dreamed of you for so long, but now that you're here, it was so worth the wait! We promise to love and support you and be the best parents that we can be!

We love you!
Mom & Dad

a baby is a little bit of
heaven
on
EARTH

TIPS Chapter 2—Photos can help you fill in the years, Chapter 3—Put yourself in the picture, Chapter 4—Simplify / Get close, Chapter 5—Keep it simple / Journaling makes the best decoration

PRODUCTS USED Delight Tone-on-Tone Paper, Cement Cardstock Paper, White Ruled Paper, Expressions of Precious Boy Vellum Accents, Classic Fine-Tip Pen Set, Foam Squares, Frosted Photo Splits, Love Struck Maker

I LOVE ICE CREAM. Clearly, this layout is all about the photos. It's such a simple moment, but this one moment captures and represents a whole stage of life. Get down, eye-to-eye, and move in close. And, just like Ulrica said in chapter 4, give a child something to do while you're shooting and you'll get engaged, active, natural photos. So cute!

love at first bite

your first cone

TIPS Chapter 4—Get close / Be patient / Give kids something to do, Chapter 5—Keep it simple

PRODUCTS USED Cheerful Tone-on-Tone Paper, Cardstock Paper (Clay, Cranberry, Red, White), Black Simple ABC/123 Stickers, Custom Cutting System with Circle Patterns and Jumbo Circle Pattern, Circle Maker, Sweet Heart Maker, Emmascript (font)

READY FOR OUR MIRACLE. I love the way this layout brings to life Ulrica's suggestion in chapter 4 that you look for all the little details you can photograph. In this baby layout, there is no baby to be in the pictures. That's the point. So each of these sweet little close-ups shows off just how ready and waiting Mom and Dad are.

TIPS Chapter 3—Do your homework, Chapter 4—Look for little details / Simplify

PRODUCTS USED Cardstock Paper (Cloud, Cranberry, Espresso, White), Basic Decorative Cardstock Shapes, Swirly Monogram Stickers (Brown, White), Brown Swirly ABC/123 Stickers, Classic Fine-tip Pen Set, Sweet Heart Maker, Scallop Circle Maker

SUNDAY BRUNCH. There's a lot to like in this layout. It's clean and simple. The photos are adorable. And the quote gets right to the point. But the thing that really catches my eye about this layout is the way Mom and Dad trade off and take turns. This is such an important point: If you're the family photographer, please make sure you find a way to get yourself into the picture! Those kids are going to want to remember what you looked like too.

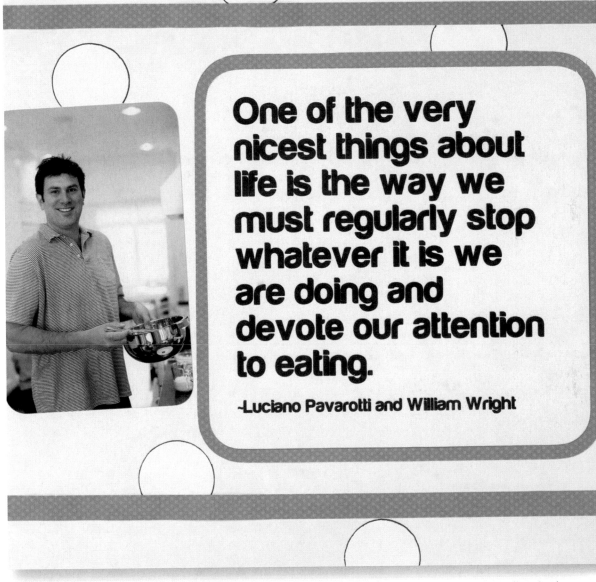

One of the very nicest things about life is the way we must regularly stop whatever it is we are doing and devote our attention to eating.

-Luciano Pavarotti and William Wright

TIPS Chapter 4—Get close / Give kids something to do / Be patient, Chapter 5—Journaling is the best decoration

PRODUCTS USED Cheerful Tone-on-Tone Paper, White Cardstock Paper, White Simple ABC/123 Stickers, Basic Fine-Tip Pen Set, Custom Cutting System with Jumbo Wavy Square Pattern, Circle Maker, Love Struck Maker, Corner Maker, Harabara Bold (font)

PICNIC PLEASURES. One of the things that makes this family look so comfortable is also one of the things that makes these photos look so great. They've found a nice, shady spot on a sunny afternoon! Remember when you're shooting that direct sunlight, especially high, mid-day sunlight, can create harsh shadows.

simple pleasures

I really love these carefree days when we have nothing planned but to spend the day together! Our days are so scheduled trying to keep up with our jobs and the boys' activities, these rare moments are _extra_ special.

TIPS Chapter 3—Use your handwriting, Chapter 4—Look for little details / Screen the sun / Color-coordinate your shots / Give kids something to do

PRODUCTS USED Discover Tone-on-Tone Paper, Discover Paper Buttons, Black & White Title Stickers, White Cardstock Paper, Basic Fine-Tip Pen Set, Foam Squares, Tearing Tool

This is my favorite get together. It refreshes me. Good books initiate great conversations. Good friends – good food. When is the next one?

WE READ. With an ensemble cast like this book club, this layout has a lot to cover. The big, 10x8 group photo on the left-hand page is a perfect way to introduce everyone. And it provides a beautiful visual anchor that balances out the series of smaller shots on the right-hand page. These photos also present a comfortable combination of posed and candid photos.

TIPS Chapter 3—Put yourself in the picture, Chapter 4—Look for little details / Get close, Chapter 5—Focus on the photos

PRODUCTS USED Reminisce Tone-on-Tone Paper, Reminisce Designer-Print Paper, Reminisce Paper Ribbon, Cardstock Paper (Black, White), White Ruled Paper, White Simple ABC/123 Stickers, Basic Fine-Tip Pen Set, Tag Maker, Scallop Circle Maker

The first dance! Seems like just yesterday we were getting ready for the first dance recital. I wondered what you were most looking forward to ... and you surprised me by saying that "getting ready and hanging out with friends" was the best part.

GIRLS NIGHT. I love the way this layout uses so many photos to really convey the mood of the moment. See the way the right-hand page balances the six smaller photos with the one, slightly larger photo? And take a look at the journaling. This mom's asking questions and getting surprising answers!

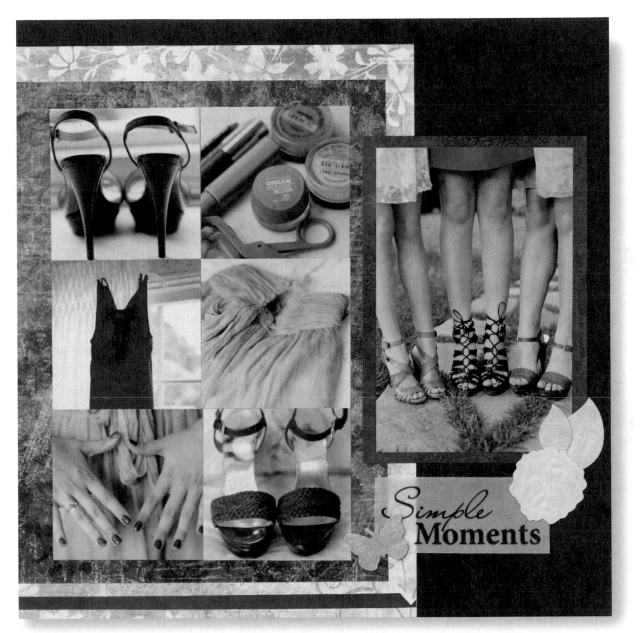

TIPS Chapter 3—Be curious, Chapter 4—Look for little details, Chapter 5—Focus on the photos

PRODUCTS USED Hummingbird Paper & Photo Mats, Hummingbird Embellishments, Hummingbird Expressions of Life Vellum Accents, Delight Paper Ribbon, White Ruled Paper, Espresso Cardstock Paper, White Swirly ABC/123 Stickers, Basic Fine-Tip Pen Set, Frosted Photo Splits

FALL FAMILY. The photos in this layout really illustrate what Ulrica was talking about in chapter 4 when she recommended shooting vertically. When you turn that camera on its side, you instantly eliminate almost all background clutter because you've gotten rid of the space on each side of your subject. I think it really helps you keep the emphasis where you want it.

Happiness comes of the capacity
to feel deeply, to enjoy simply,
to think freely, to risk life,
   to be needed.   ~Storm Jameson

The day for our family reunion
turned out to be a beautiful
fall day.
As always, I moved around from
group to group snapping photos
of family.
What a nice surprise it was
when my Aunt Sue insisted
that I be in some of the
photos for a change!

I absolutely love what
she captured!

TIPS Chapter 3—Put yourself in the picture, Chapter 4—Screen the sun / Shoot vertically, Chapter 5—Keep it simple

PRODUCTS USED 12x12 Natural Scrapbook Pages, Hummingbird Paper & Photo Mats, Hummingbird Embellishments, Classic Fine-Tip Pen Set

I asked the girls what they loved, liked, etc … and they mentioned they were scared about growing up and being apart. They've been the best of friends since they were little. I assured them that true friends will always be close … no matter what the distance is in miles.

TREASURE EVERY MOMENT. In chapter 5 I talk about tearing your decorations rather than getting all fussy about measurements. This layout shows a cute spin on that. Look at the way the paper ribbon is used on the left-hand page to frame the photo. Just roll out the ribbon, crease some sharp folds, and snip it off when you get back to where you started. And if your joint doesn't match up perfectly, add a butterfly or a flower on top. See? Simple!

It's the **little things** that make life *beautiful.*

Treasure *every* moment

TIPS Chapter 3—Be curious, Chapter 4—Simplify / Get close, Chapter 5—Tear it up

PRODUCTS USED Hummingbird Paper & Photo Mats, Hummingbird Embellishments, Hummingbird Paper Ribbon, Black & White Title Stickers, White Cardstock Paper, Classic Fine-Tip Pen Set, Foam Squares, Corner Maker

Just watching. them interact with each other reminds me of my sister and I. I wonder what little (or big!)

Family is Forever

secrets they'll share as the years go by.

For now, watching them grow and love each other is enough.

FAMILY IS FOREVER. These photos just crack me up! And I think what I like best about them is how natural they are. This is what Ulrica had in mind in chapter 4 when she talked about being patient. You could shoot, shoot, shoot all day and you might happen to get these shots. Or you could watch and wait and get into position so that when the moment's right, you're ready!

TIPS Chapter 3—Put yourself in the picture, Chapter 4—Get close / Be patient, Chapter 5—Focus on the photos

PRODUCTS USED Reminisce Tone-on-Tone Paper, Reminisce Title Stickers, White Cardstock Paper, Classic Fine-Tip Pen Set, Corner Maker, Sweet Heart Maker

Our family loves to spend time at the beach, but our moments as a family are never captured as I am always the one behind the camera. On this day my girlfriend Susan agreed to join us, so that she could help us capture all our family's fun and memorable moments. The photos turned out exactly as I had hoped! Thanks Susan!

THANKFUL FOR YOU. In chapter 5 I talk about how much fun it can be to stack and layer your decorations. This layout shows some great examples of how to do that without getting complicated or time consuming. The paper buttons, flowers and ribbon all come from coordinating packs, so the colors all match. Once you're comfortable with that, you're free to just pick your pieces and find combinations you like.

TIPS Chapter 3—Tell the backstory, Chapter 4—Rule of thirds, Chapter 5—Focus on the photos / Stack and layer / Tear it up

PRODUCTS USED 12x12 Black Scrapbook Pages, Simply Beautiful Tone-on-Tone Paper, Simply Beautiful Paper Ribbon, Simply Beautiful Paper Tags, Simply Beautiful Paper Flowers, Black & White Title Stickers, White Ruled Paper, Black Simple ABC/123 Stickers, Basic Fine-Tip Pen Set, Foam Squares, Tearing Tool

Sweet Treats

Emma and Gracie wanted to surprise Daddy with cupcakes for his birthday. They picked their favorite candies to decorate them.

SWEET TREATS. Being a parent means giving kids the experiences that will help them take on bigger projects as they grow. When you can make that learning fun and then capture that fun forever for them ... that's a big success!

The girls helped dump in the ingredients, stir the batter and fill the liners. They could hardly wait for the cupcakes to cool so they could begin decorating. We were just starting when we got a surprise; Daddy came home early! The girls both yelled, "No Daddy, don't look!" But, they really couldn't wait to show him their creations.

TIPS Chapter 2—Use photo albums to teach kids independence, Chapter 3—Tell the backstory, Chapter 4—Look for little details / Get close / Give kids something to do, Chapter 5—Keep it simple

PRODUCTS USED Delight Tone-on-Tone Paper, Delight Paper Ribbon, White Ruled Paper, Cement Cardstock Paper, Brown Sophisticate ABC/123 Stickers, Classic Fine-Tip Pen Set

FARMERS' MARKET. A picture can be worth a thousand words. And, as much as I love journaling, sometimes it's even better to let the photos speak for themselves! That's where a quick journaling shortcut like a list works perfectly.

All of our favorite finds for the day...

1 Fabulous Jewelry

FARMERS' MARKET HERE TODAY

RAW INSPIRATION

2 A ring that is made for nana

3 Ripe, juicy strawberries!

TIPS Chapter 3—Take journaling shortcuts, Chapter 4—Look for little details, Chapter 5—Focus on the photos / Stack and layer

PRODUCTS USED Cheerful Title Stickers, Cheerful Paper Ribbon, Cardstock Paper (White, Black), Basic Fine-Tip Pen Set, Corner Maker, Petal Multi-Maker, Circle Maker

STARTING PRESCHOOL. Your child's new preschool teacher is demonstrating a wonderful point about responsibility – just the sort of thing you might want to leverage and reinforce at home! With this bright, colorfully fun page, they'll always be able to look back on the work, the teamwork, the reasons and the rewards.

TIPS Chapter 2—Use albums to show children real-life stories, Chapter 4—Look for little details / Get close, Chapter 5—Journaling is the best decoration

PRODUCTS USED Cheerful School Additions, Gray Cardstock Paper, Black Simple ABC/123 Stickers, Basic Fine-Tip Pen Set

Lexi wants to cut her hair and have bangs - just to be like him!

They would die to meet Justin in person!

THE BEST THINGS. Sure, acknowledging the girls' latest teen idol in your album isn't the same as commemorating some kind of epic achievement or milestone event. But it's cute little moments like these that will mark the passage of time for these girls. And someday, when their own daughters get a little goofy over the latest sensation, they'll be able to share just how much they loved Justin (and just how much Grandma loved Rob Lowe!).

Wouldn't they make a cute couple?

The *best things* in life aren't ~~things~~ - they are FRIENDS.

Emily and Lexi had been waiting for weeks for the latest issue of their teen magazine to come out. They knew that this month would be featuring Justin Bieber, their latest heart throb! I'm pretty sure that the store hadn't even gotten them out on the shelves when they grabbed them. When they got back home they read the book from cover to cover and "oohed" and "aahed" over all of the photos of him! I remember when I was their age... any magazine with Rob Lowe in it... I just had to have!

TIPS Chapter 3—Put yourself in the picture, Chapter 4—Simplify / Shoot vertically / Get close, Chapter 5—Go naked!

PRODUCTS USED 12x12 Natural Scrapbook Pages, Expressions of Those We Love Vellum Accents, Basic Fine-Tip Pen Set, Frosted Photo Splits

simple pleasures

When we get together for our book club, it's not just about coming together to discuss the book chosen for the month. And, although we love to visit and catch up on what's going on in each of our lives, it's not just about that either. It's about the food! We love to eat and the menu for our book club gatherings has become quite elaborate over the years; each trying to be more creative and to out to the others!

SIMPLE PLEASURES. The title sticker says it all here. This layout is fantastically simple and really demonstrates the fact that quick, photo-and-journaling layouts can be beautiful! These women have books to read, lives to live, food to eat, friends to catch up with ... and albums to enjoy. Who says you can't have it all?

August Menu: Hot Bacon Bites
               Cheesy Salmon Puffs
               Little Link Wraps
               Spinach-Cheese Triangles
               Fresh Fruit
               Orange Juice Spritzer

TIPS Chapter 4—Look for little details / Get close, Chapter 5—Go naked!

PRODUCTS USED 12x12 White Scrapbook Pages, Black & White Title Stickers, White Ruled Paper, Basic Fine-Tip Pen Set

GAME ON. Want one simple trick for when you're ready to turn the corner and start making some fun scrapbook layouts? Try rounding the corners. I don't know why, but that one simple step just gives everything a smooth, easy feeling. I don't do it all the time, but on some layouts it's just the thing. A Corner Maker is an inexpensive little tool you'll end up using for years.

Next to soccer, baseball is his second favorite passion, just like daddy!

Just like my dad!

Sports are my life!

a smile happens in a flash, but the memory can last a lifetime. —unknown

TIPS Chapter 4—Color-coordinate your shots / Get close, Chapter 5—Keep it simple

PRODUCTS USED Cheerful Designer-Print Paper, Cheerful Title Stickers, Cardstock Paper (Clay, Cranberry, Deep Blue), Basic Fine-Tip Pen Set, White Simple ABC/123 Stickers, White Simple Monogram Stickers, Foam Squares, Custom Cutting System with Circle Patterns, Corner Maker, Embossed Star Maker, Circle Maker, Galaxy Micro Maker

Apple Picking on the Farm

Picking apples at the farm always brings back so many memories of going out to the u-picks by our home when I was little. Mom would pack us kids in the car and drive out to the farms with buckets in tow. We would pick apples, berries, nectarines, and peaches.

APPLE PICKING. The photos in this layout just come together to create one completely wonderful picture! This is what Ulrica meant in chapter 4 when she talked about looking for little details to capture. Sure, the focus is on picking apples. But the backstory is the flood of memories it brings back for Mom. And all the supporting photographs help capture that.

Peaches were my favorite! They always tasted so much better than the ones from the store! Afterwards we would take them home and either can them or make preserves. Almost always Mom would hold some back to make a fresh pie out of! I love that going out to the farm with you kids can bring all these great memories back to me!

TIPS Chapter 3—Tell the backstory / Put yourself in the picture, Chapter 4—Look for little details / Get close, Chapter 5—Focus on the photos

PRODUCTS USED StoryBook Creator Plus Software, Day-to-Day Digital Kit, Newsroom Digital Alpha Set

It's Father's Day 2010, and Priya couldn't wait to celebrate this special day with her daddy. She made a special card and helped bake his favorite cookies. I asked her what her favorite thing about Daddy was. She said that she loves how he pushes her so high on the swing set! Then, she asked me what my favorite thing was about her Daddy. And of course, without any hesitation at all, I told her that I loved her Daddy because he loves her so very much! And of course, because he is such an absolutely amazing, kind, wonderful and caring husband.

To laugh often & love much... to appreciate Beauty to find the BEST in others, to GIVE this to yourself... this is to have SUCCEEDED. - Ralph Waldo Emerson

FATHER'S DAY. For this Father's Day layout, Mom has clearly done her homework. The photos are fantastic, and I'm sure the day itself was wonderful. She could have just left the page at that. But by taking a few minutes to get Priya's thoughts on Dad, this page becomes so much more.

TIPS Chapter 3—Do your homework, Chapter 4—Shoot vertically / Rule of thirds / Get close, Chapter 5—Focus on the photos / Journaling is the best decoration

PRODUCTS USED Reminisce Designer-Print Paper, Reminisce Paper Flowers, Black & White Title Stickers, Cement Cardstock Paper, Spargo Ruled Paper, Basic Fine-Tip Pen Set, Foam Squares

You are only a few days old son, yet it is hard to imagine life without you in it! Your soft little cry, your baby smell, your handsome face, they are all a part of our life now and I wouldn't have it any other way! I can tell I am going to love being your Dad!

1ST DAY HOME. Easy does it! Before you know it, they'll be wrestling in the backyard. But, for now, Dad's being very careful. My favorite thing about this layout is the way the series of "highlight" photos is balanced by the one larger color photo and journaling. Beautiful!

1st Day Home

TIPS Chapter 3—Put yourself in the picture, Chapter 4—Shoot vertical / Get close, Chapter 5—Focus on the photos

PRODUCTS USED StoryBook Creator Plus Software, Discover Digital Baby Boy Additions, Sewing Room Baby Boy Digital Embellishments, CAC Futura Casual and Pooh (fonts)

HE ♥ LOVES PANCAKES!

Jake adores pancakes. He'll eat them for breakfast, lunch, and supper. He likes them plain. He likes them with maple syrup. He likes them with homemade whip cream. He just loves pancakes!

HE LOVES PANCAKES. Hello? Who doesn't?! This is the kind of quirky, everyday moment that will make your album extra special years from now. Sure, you'll want to capture Jake's first day of kindergarten and all his fantastic birthday parties. But someday, someone will open this album and smile at the flood of memories as they ask, "Hey Jake! Remember your infamous 'pancake stage'?"

TIPS Chapter 4—Shoot vertically / Get close, Chapter 5—Focus on the photos

PRODUCTS USED StoryBook Creator Plus Software, Cheerful Digital Birthday Additions, Base '02 (font)

CONCLUSION

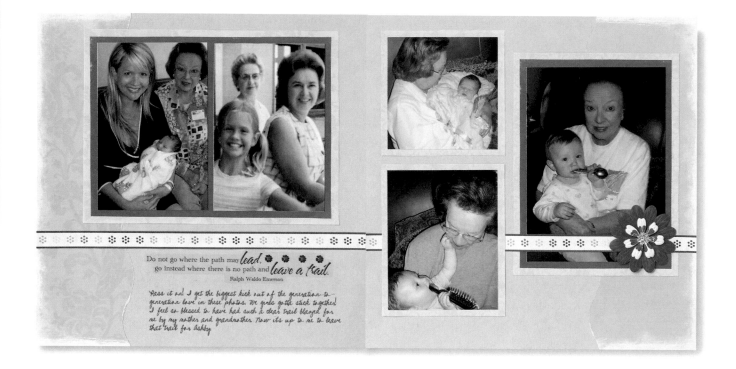

Do not go where the path may *lead*, go instead where there is no path and *leave a trail.*
Ralph Waldo Emerson

Pass it on! I get the biggest kick out of the generation to generation love in these photos. We girls gotta stick together! I feel so blessed to have had such a clear trail blazed for me by my mother and grandmother. Now its up to me to leave that trail for Ashby.

THE NEXT STEP IS YOURS. You just need to find your own path.

I believe with all my heart that documenting your life and loves is one of the most productive ways you can spend your valuable time. The pictures above remind me that scrapbooking is a gift that can be passed down from one generation to the next – both in the actual books and in the love of capturing and preserving memories. I've inherited my mother's albums. But I've also inherited the love of making my own. Someday I wish the same for my children.

Some of the points Dr. Condrell made when I spoke with him surprised me. But most of what he said I already knew in my heart because I've lived it every day of my life. I've felt the love, support and hope that photo albums can deliver to a child. I've felt that connection to family. I know who I am because I remember where I came from, and I've seen what came before me.

You have the power to create an album of hope – for a child, for a group or organization, for a dream…. You have the stories. You can take the photos. And now you have tips and strategies to make those even better. The problem is actually doing something with them. (For the faint-hearted, with stacks of photos and little time, this is where things can start to look daunting.)

This is the spot where a mentor, like a Creative Memories Consultant* really can be a blessing. Sit down face-to-face and talk about your options. Share your goals and dreams. And explain your fears as well.

Together, you can find a style and the tools that will let you get the job done. Sure, this book can give you suggestions. Magazines and websites can show you ideas. But no one can tell you what your pages should look like. That's for you to discover.

Just remember, photo albums don't have to be time consuming. The pages my mom made that included nothing more than photos, bits of memorabilia and her handwriting mean more to me than any fancy work of art.

So put your photos down and write from the heart. That's what people will remember.

I'll be cheering you on!

*If you don't have a Creative Memories Consultant,
you can find one on their website at www.creativememories.com.

BONUS!

Find exclusive layout instructions at
http://projectcenter.creativememories.com/nancy.

Use username **FullOfLayouts** and password **Link2Layouts.**

HUMMINGBIRD SERIES

When I started teaming up with Creative Memories I dreamed of products that were both beautiful and accessible. I wanted pieces that might inspire a person to begin creating albums. And I wanted pieces that would make it easy and quick for the beginner and busy parent.

This is the Hummingbird Series from Creative Memories. A dream come true.

You can see more and find a Creative Memories Consultant of your own at www.creativememories.com!

ABOUT

Nancy O'Dell is an Emmy Award-winning journalist, entrepreneur, producer and philanthropist. One of the country's most respected and well-known entertainment hosts, she was on the original *Access Hollywood* team and anchored for 13 years. She has contributed to CBS's *The Early Show* as well as NBC's *Today Show* and *Dateline*. As co-host of Oprah Winfrey's premiere primetime show, *Your Own Show*, on the new OWN network, Nancy is fulfilling her dream of working with Oprah. With 20 years of live television experience, Nancy has hosted countless specials, including multiple *Emmy Awards Red Carpet* shows as well as *The Live Golden Globes Arrivals Special* and *The Tournament of Roses Parade* for nine years in a row. Nancy's first book "*FULL OF LIFE: Mom-to-Mom Tips I Wish Someone Told Me When I Was Pregnant*," debuted in 2009 and instantly became a best-selling gift title. As a designer, Nancy has her own line of outdoor furniture called "Red Carpet by Nancy O'Dell" and a new line of scrapbooking products with Creative Memories. She is a self-described "scrapbooking fiend" who scraps "anything and everything." Nancy is a co-host of the annual MDA telethon and, with MDA, founded Betty's Battle, a charity named in honor of her mother, who passed away from ALS in 2008. She lives in Los Angeles with her husband, her two stepsons and her daughter.

Kenneth Condrell, Ph.D. is a child psychologist, family therapist, and author who has been in private practice for nearly 40 years. He is also a Clinical Assistant Professor in the Department of Psychiatry, School of Medicine, at the State University of New York at Buffalo, and he makes frequent guest appearances on national TV to address issues relating to children and families. As his family's official photographer and scrapbooker (and with nine grandchildren!) he has plenty to scrap about.

Ulrica Wihlborg was born and raised in Sweden before moving to San Francisco. Her photographs reflect the signature Scandinavian aesthetic of simplicity with their clean, organic lines. When she's not behind the camera, Ulrica writes about celebrity happenings as an assistant editor at *People* magazine. She lives in Los Angeles with her husband and their two young sons.

Dave Kirchner is an award-winning freelance writer who first fell under the spell of scrapbooking when he became part of the team that launched Creative Memories' *Lasting Moments* magazine. His work has appeared in *Better Homes and Gardens*, *Midwest Living* and other national magazines. If you don't count the time he wrote about how to style hair for Barbie dolls, *Full of Love* is his first celebrity memoir. He pounds the keyboard (headphones on) in Des Moines, Iowa.